"I have known Norm Wakefield for many years. He has become a role model to me. Norm doesn't just speak the truth; he lives the truth."

—Josh McDowell
bestselling author and international speaker

"The material in Norm Wakefield's Living In God's Presence has impacted men and women's lives through Norm's gifted teaching. He has the heart of a shepherd and a love for the Chief Shepherd. You will find that his faithful teaching of the Word of God will help you discover the heart of our heavenly Father."

—Darryl DelHousaye
president, Phoenix Seminary

"Having a true knowledge of God and knowing who you are as a child of God is the greatest determinant of the Christian's mental health, identity, security, and significance. I can't think of another Christian leader better equipped to impart that knowledge to you than Dr. Norm Wakefield."

—Neil T. Anderson
bestselling author and founder of Freedom in Christ Ministries

LIVING
IN
GOD'S PRESENCE

Also by Norm Wakefield

The Joyful Dad

Men Are From Israel, Women Are from Moab

Between the Words

Who Gives a R.I.P. About Sin

LIVING

IN

GOD'S PRESENCE

Dr. Norm Wakefield

WALKING C CARNIVAL

"Make Readers Happy."

Loveland, Colorado

Living in God's Presence
ISBN 978-1-939953-02-5

Published by Walking Carnival, an imprint of Nappaland Communications Inc.

Visit us on the web at: WalkingCarnival.com

1 2 3 4 5 / 2016 2015 2014 2013

DEDICATION

This book is dedicated to all the students and friends who have helped me discover and refine the insights that I share in here. You have challenged me, encouraged me, been patient with me, loved me, and motivated me to grow. Thank you!

N.W.

"THE LORD IS GRACIOUS AND MERCIFUL,
SLOW TO ANGER AND
ABOUNDING IN STEADFAST LOVE."

—PSALM 145:8

CONTENTS

INTRODUCTION

I confess, I'm an addict. I'm addicted to food. I have a love/hate relationship with pot luck meals. Aah, how I love to walk down the serving line and see all those delicious items. I can't resist trying some of everything. And when my plate is emptied I feel compelled to go back for more. When that's finished I still feel that I am missing something that I should have savored.

But then I hate the feeling that I've made a glutton of myself and will regret what I read when I step on the scales the next morning. So I resolve that I won't do it again. But when the next pot luck rolls around I'm back at the head of the line eager to sample all the goodies.

I've endured the shame of my addiction since I was in grade school. My Grandmother Learn was the original pot luck lady. She knew how to load a table with all sorts of tasty morsels that would appeal to a boy with big eyes and an even bigger appetite. When she called us for dinner I was there in a flash. How I loved to savor all those different flavors. I'd stuff myself until I couldn't eat any more. Then I'd waddle over to the couch and lay down to let the goodies digest. Those days laid the foundation for my food addiction.

So what's your addiction? What's that craving that you have difficulty resisting? What is the urge you can't control?

You might as well be honest because I'm convinced that everyone has some kind of inordinate desire. Most of us frown on the Big Three. Drugs, pornography, and alcohol are probably at the top of the list, but what about being a workaholic? Or addicted to gossip? Or compulsive buying? Even addicted to TV. Yes, the list goes on and on.

I once knew a woman who was addicted to buying clothes. It drove her husband crazy because she would do it when he wasn't looking. The next thing he knew was there wasn't enough money in the checking account to pay the bills. He finally took money away from her and gave her an allowance! It was the only way to restrain her addiction.

Behind all such things that seek to seduce us is a insatiable craving for something. Something that can't be satisfied once for all. Some powerful yearning that won't go away. The word "addiction" suggests that no matter how much I indulge my appetite I'm never satisfied. I have to go back for another "fix."

Behind all addictions is a hunger; a longing for intimacy. We long to have something that will make us feel satisfied. Something that will stop the craving. But I would submit that basic to this powerful desire is a powerful longing for intimacy with our heavenly Father.

We have an inborn need for intimacy.

I'm convinced that whether a person is a follower of Christ or not we all have a subconscious longing for fulfillment that is rooted in our being created in the image of God. We are drawn to be fulfilled by only what he can supply.

A LITTLE PERSONAL HISTORY

It took me years to recognize the true source of my addictive hunger. My early history could be described as a longing to be cherished, a longing to be loved unconditionally by someone. My family didn't provide an environment where that happened. This isn't a complaint against my mother and father. The stresses and strains of their relationship didn't allow such intimacy for a flock of seven children. I was the fourth of four boys so there wasn't anything I could do that three older brothers couldn't do better — and they liked to remind me of that. It also seemed — from my perspective — that I was the one who was always getting into trouble.

So I looked for ways to fill my emotional tank. I wanted to be special to someone. I wanted to be cherished. I tried to gain a sense of intimacy but it never worked because all the ways I sought to satisfy them were illegitimate and never left me with inner contentment.

When I was twelve years old Mr. Rice, my Sunday school teacher told me about Jesus Christ and his passionate love for me. One Sunday I bowed my head and received God's gift of eternal life. I've been grateful for that event for over a half century.

But, it didn't fill the void. Not because God's love is inadequate, but because I didn't understand my true need and the nature of my heavenly Father and his beloved Son, Jesus Christ. For far too many years I felt that his expectations of me were like those my earthly father placed on me. I was never able to satisfy my father's expectations so why should I believe that my heavenly Father was any different? I believed that I was a disappointment to him. So the real source of contentment was never met. It was always there, but I didn't recognize it.

Now I understand that God really is Heaven's Lover, pursuing his children with a relentless passion to bring us into that place where his love, his grace, and his care is more than enough. I now know that to paraphrase an old hymn, there is a place of quiet rest near to the heart of our Lord. There is a place of peace and soul contentment where the stresses and trials of the world cannot destroy.

As I've come to discover and experience the indescribable Father-love of our Lord I've found that his ability to fill our lives with a profound peace and contentment is genuine and lasting. I feel sad that so many never experience the passionate heart of our Lord. But I've had a good measure of joy guiding friends and students through a process whereby they begin to grasp the profound Father-child relationship that is waiting to be received.

Discovering the rich, multifaceted nature of our heavenly Father is like exploring the Grand Canyon. I live in Arizona and have visited this phenomena several times. I've stood on the rim and gazed out upon that breathtaking, spectacular sight. Every time I go back I am reminded again that it is so vast, so multi-colored, so long, deep and wide that I could spend my entire life exploring it. And I realize that I can't begin to tell others of this fullness. They must experience it for themselves. But I can invite them to come to the Canyon with me, or I can give them directions how to get there. In the same way I want to encourage others to see the panorama of our Lord's amazing heart for us. If I can be a guide to point the way I will be gratified for the privilege.

ADDICTED TO GOD

We typically define addiction in a negative way. But its root meaning speaks of a strong desire to be fulfilled in some way. I believe that we were created with a basic positive addiction. The Psalmist challenges us to "taste and see that the Lord is good. Blessed is the man who takes refuge in him!" (Psalm 34:8). Later he says, "How sweet are your words to my taste, sweeter than honey to my mouth!" (Psalm 119:103). It seems to me that we were created with this positive addiction to hunger and thirst for an intimate relationship with our beloved Lord. So what went wrong that we lost that and are now at the mercy of mis-guided hungers and thirsts?

The evil one is very clever. He knows that if he can switch a substitute for the real thing then he can gain control of our lives. One thing I've learned is that he takes our legitimate needs and attaches them to illegitimate ones. He whispers, "I know how great your need is. I sympathize with you. Let me suggest an easy, fun way to meet it."

I have a valid need for nourishment. But I am tempted to overindulge and become a glutton. We all need to feel secure, but we can seek everywhere but from the Great Protector. We were created to be fruitful and productive, but that can become twisted into workaholism. We need healthy relationships but we can be led into unhealthy ones to gain the approval of others. Each substitute leads us further away from fulfillment by the Eternal Source

This book is about the ultimate addiction; an incurable, wonderful longing for intimacy with the God of heaven. I want to point you in the direction of the supremely satisfying relationship. My goal is to help you discover what you really are looking for. If you will embark on this journey under the guidance of the Holy Spirit I'm certain that you will see our kind, compassionate Lord more clearly. I hope that you will see how you have been misled and may even be wandering down a hopeless path.

Think of this book as a journey to explore the heart of our beloved heavenly Father. The early chapters will help you think through how you formed your concept of God. All of us have received input from a variety of sources and many of them were not accurate. If someone has learned to see the Lord as a stern, no-nonsense God then he will tell us that this is what God is like. I am certain that all of us have been taught distortions about him and these distortions create a distorted relationship. Remember, *the terms, conditions or expectations of a relationship determine the nature of the relationship*. But if I've learned terms, conditions or expectations that are not what our Lord has said, my false perception will shape the relationship. I could give you countless examples of this truth seen in the lives of Christ followers that I have known.

As you move through the book you will discover what the Bible says about our heavenly Father. He is the most beautiful, loyal, kind, generous, compassionate Person that you will ever meet. He is the Father that we all have longed to experience. My prayer is that you will see him through new eyes and experience his loving presence in a way that begins to fill that insatiable longing for intimacy within you. I pray that the unquenchable thirst you have will be satisfied by the living Water.

I invite you to experience the soul satisfying Source that will fill your inner longing.

1.
INTRODUCE ME TO YOUR GOD

Today I watched Tracy, an adult child of my beloved Sovereign. She is so fearful and anxious about her life when in fact she is secure in the arms of her eternal Lord. She must not believe that she is safe from all evil. Yet he has clearly said in the Holy Book that he is a refuge, a shelter, a protector. I wonder why his children worry and fret. Why do these humans who have a sure defense under the Eternal King still get anxious and afraid. It puzzles me.

— Diary of a Puzzled Angel

WHOM SHALL I TRUST?

As much as I like a new car the process of finding and buying one is always emotionally taxing. It's been that way as long as I can remember. The heart of the problem is that I don't know whether I can trust the seller.

For many years I couldn't afford a new car so I had to look for a reliable used model. And no matter how attractive it looked and how well the engine purred, I had that nervous feeling that there was something wrong with it and I'd get stuck with a lemon. Then I'd look like a fool to my family and friends.

One factor that prompted this struggle was what I'd learned from my own dad. For one thing he was a shrewd buyer, challenging the seller with a brash boldness. I was with him one time when he laid out twelve one hundred dollar bills on the salesman's desk and said, "Do you want to sell it or don't you!" He made the deal I didn't have the guts to make.

Dad also taught me to be skeptical of the seller. His message that resonated in my mind was "Don't trust the salesman. He's out to take you for as much as he can. No matter how pleasant he is, he's doing it to make a sale. Don't believe anything he says. All he's interested in is your money!" Though he died a number of years ago that message is firmly implanted in my mind and emotions.

Another part of the issue was that I didn't think he trusted my ability to make wise decisions. So when I endeavored to make a significant purchase the anxiety would surface again. Subconsciously I'd hear my dad's words and believe that I'd make a stupid purchase and suffer the consequences.

Recently my wife and I decided to shop for a new car. I was excited about the prospect, but anxious about the process. Yes. I've had a lifetime of experience. Still when I met salesman Joe those old tapes began to cycle through my mind and I heard the still small voice saying, "Look out Norm, he's out to get you. Don't believe anything he says." Now understand, I'd done my homework concerning the reliability of the car and the trustworthiness of the dealer, but that didn't dispel that persistent worry.

I should tell you that we bought the car and it was a positive experience.

SIGN ON THE DOTTED LINE

Perhaps my experience surfaced some thoughts and feelings within you. Many of us may share similar feelings when it comes to trusting others when much is at stake. This is especially true when it comes to our Lord. We want an intimate relationship with God but we've heard a lot of conflicting statements about who he is and the way he treats people. We've been conditioned in so many ways with a variety of opinions people have about God. When someone told us about his love for us in sending Jesus Christ to die for our sins we got high hopes and responded to his invitation. But even then we kept hearing the "counsel" of others warning us not to get too excited about it, or reminding us of all that this relationship is going to cost us in the end. We've purchased the vehicle, but can't believe that the dealer will actually deliver what he promised.

We can't avoid relationships. They're an integral part of living a fulfilled, fruitful life. Even in purchasing a car a person has to relate to the salesperson. We are constantly building, sustaining or ending them and this ongoing process fills us with emotions running the gauntlet from joy, sorrow, anger, pleasure, indifference, and anticipation..

What strikes me as I reflect on this is how quickly children discover the rules of relationships. Eighteen month old Holly scowls, whines, cries and yells to indicate her displeasure and demand attention. But she also thrills her parents hearts with impish grins and giggles. As I watch two year old David and his older brother interact I can clearly see how their parents and others are training them to relate to others. Calvin, the older brother, already demonstrates interpersonal skills that will help him build satisfying relationships with others. He knows some of the basic terms essential to build and maintain healthy relationships.

Children learn how to build relationships through trial and error. As we grow older *our past experience conditions us to know what to expect in relationships*. I've shared how I confronted a problem that involved relationships. I couldn't escape that persistent internal voice of my father predicting what the terms of my relationship with automobile salesmen would be. Dad's pessimism conditioned me to think and feel anxious when in the presence of salesmen.

I know a young woman who dated a kind, warm, caring Christian man. But after a few months she ended the relationship. Her rationale was that "he was just too good to be true." Like me and the salesman, she was afraid that sooner or later some serious flaw would be revealed and then she would be disappointed. The young man really was a kind, warm, caring Christian man, but the woman had experienced disappointing letdowns in the past and couldn't believe that this one wouldn't turn out the same, so she terminated the relationship to avoid what she was sure would be a painful ending.

When I bought my new car I knew that I'd sign a contract between me and the dealership. But actually I was signing a contract to honor relationships. I was agreeing with the owners of the dealership that I could be counted on to fulfill my financial responsibilities and the owners were agreeing that they would provide a reliable automobile and would honor warranties that they promised to fulfill. *All significant relationships are spoken or unspoken contracts to honor certain spoken or unspoken commitments.*

I am a seminary professor. I respect and value my students. One way we maintain healthy relationships is by entering into a contract with each other at the beginning of a specific course. I agree to be a certain kind of person and provide the most effective kind of classroom experience I can and the student agrees to act responsibly in certain ways. These agreements help us maintain a warm friendship inside and outside the classroom.

But there's a second factor to consider. Even when we have accurate facts before us we sometimes experience a gnawing feeling of uncertainty or anxiousness in relationships. This is frequently due to the fact that our childhood perceptions of relationship dynamics are rooted in our feelings, not on facts. Young children don't have the capacity to think relationships through intellectually so they interpret them on the basis of their feelings. When my granddaughter, Alexa, was little she took a long while warming up to me because I wear a beard. Her apprehension was not based on facts, but on her discomfort with someone who doesn't look "normal" to her.

What throws us off as adults is that those underlying feelings are influencing us, and they don't necessarily follow logic. Nevertheless, they're true to our inner perspective and usually won't disappear by intellectual argument.

WILL THE REAL GOD PLEASE STAND UP

A popular show in the early days of television consisted of three individuals who were presented before a panel as having a unique occupation or life circumstance. The panel's task was to discern which of the three was the real person and which were impostors. I've thought of this situation when individuals describe their perception of the true and living God. I remember a preacher who preached a sermon entitled, "Your God is My Devil!" His point was that the harsh, demanding "God" that many presented was a more accurate portrayal of Satan.

I assume that you, my friend, would like to experience a more intimate relationship with our heavenly Father and his Son, Jesus Christ. For many it is a frustrating venture that never seems to bear positive fruit. Intimacy always seems such an elusive goal. We read new books and sermons, and try new "strategies," but little if any progress occurs.

You may be like many individuals I've known who feel a hunger for a closer connection with the Lord. It may be helpful to remember that *developing an intimate, meaningful relationship with our Lord is based on the same underlying principles that shape any relationship.* What we fail to realize is that what we've come to believe and feel about relationships with others underlies and shapes our relationship with God. You probably noticed right away how my anxiety about dealing with a salesperson was rooted in what I'd heard and felt from my dad and others around me. In the same way others have significantly shaped our beliefs and feelings about knowing our Lord. These internal "voices" are consciously or unconsciously instructing us. So this all-important relationship is rooted in what we've come to believe about relationships in general and what we've been told about God by others. But we don't always stop and identify how others have shaped it intellectually and emotionally, and whether what they've said is actually true.

Consider this question:

Who has significantly shaped the emotional and intellectual content of your relationship with God?

(Before you continue reading pause for a couple of minutes and reflect on this question. It will help you to relate what you're reading to your life).

I recently went into a sign shop to get a new sign for the condominium association where I live. I was surprised to see a young woman working there that I knew from the fitness center I attend. She had impressed me as a cheerful, friendly person. During the conversation I asked her where she attended church. Her response was very straightforward.

"I don't attend any church. I grew up as a (her denomination) and the brand of religion I experienced was harsh, demanding and judgmental. I decided that I didn't need that kind of God. I don't intend to talk about church or Christianity!"

I left the sign shop feeling sad. The god she experienced in that church is not the heavenly Father that I've discovered throughout the Bible. I yearned for her to discover the beloved Lord that I know but the pain from her past had created an impenetrable barrier.

Let me pose a problem for you. Imagine that you heard a knock on your door. When you open the door you are confronted with three individuals. Each claims to be your heavenly Father. Could you recognize the real one? "Father" number one is dressed in a perfectly pressed suit and speaks in a loud, booming voice. He never smiles and his eyes are piercing. He says that he is the Lord of heaven and earth and is not pleased with the way you've been conducting yourself. He reminds you that you've neglected reading your Bible and prayer, haven't tithed regularly, and have not witnessed to anyone this week. "I've come to warn you that you'd better get your act together," he says sternly.

"Father" number two seems very laid back and unconcerned. He looks around the house and seems distracted. He seems more interested in more "important" people. He asks you if he can use your phone to call Billy Graham. During the time he's in your house he never engages in a conversation with you. You ask him how you can know him better. He hands you the Bible and says "Read this."

"Father" number three steps forward and places his hand on your shoulder. His smile radiates warmth that takes you off guard. "I've been looking forward to this time with much joy," he says. "I think of you constantly and know that you're troubled by your relationship with me. Why don't we sit down and talk together. You're very important to me and I want to help you grow."

Relax. The goal of this exercise is not to select the right answer. It's to help you recognize that whichever "Father" you chose was influenced by people and experiences in your life, and you probably have never thought through whether these are true representations of this all important person

As a starting point I want you to recognize that experiencing intimacy with our heavenly Father *is not fulfilling a contract*, but it is an interactive relationship in which each side needs to understand each other. In order to accomplish this we need to be able to accurately discern the answers to these questions.

1. What is the truth about this God who's inviting me into this unique relationship?

Who told me who he is and what he's like? How can I be certain that the person who told me about the Lord has an accurate perception of him? What underlying emotions towards this person are rooted in past unhealthy life experiences?

Unfortunately most of us have a very limited, scattered view of our beloved Father. We've picked up bits and pieces from a variety of reliable and unreliable sources. Just because a person is a preacher, Sunday school teacher or "authority" doesn't mean he or she is representing our Lord accurately (You might be surprised by the number of people who talk as though they're authorities on God, but who have no personal, intimate relationship with him. Even preachers can preach Bible messages without an intimate relationship with our heavenly Father).

2. How does God this view relationship?

Is he eager for it, or reluctant, feeling that he's being forced into something against his will? Is our Lord looking for slaves to bow down before him to salve his ego? Or, does he love us with a warm, intimate love that the most caring person could ever manifest?

In my own experience I felt that my heavenly Father had been forced into a relationship with me against his better judgment. It was as though he'd got stuck with me and now had to put up with someone whose life was in disorder and I was giving my heavenly Father a migraine headache.

3. What are the two of us bringing to this relationship?

What am I expecting of my Lord and what is he expecting of me? Are my expectations consistent with what the Bible actually teaches? Do I know positively what his expectations are of me? Where did I learn them? Are they what the Bible actually teaches, or what others have said?

For years I thought that my Lord had expectations of me that I could never achieve. Then I began to look more closely at what the Bible said and discovered that he had never placed those expectations on our relationship.

I've also learned to examine my own expectations of him — and myself — and see if they are consistent with what the Bible teaches. And I've discovered that whenever one of Father's children gets these issues clarified it leads to a sweeter, more intimate relationship.

SEPARATING THE WHEAT FROM THE CHAFF

Relationships are the stuff of life. But we've consciously and unconsciously assumed certain rules about relationships and as we enter into a relationship with our heavenly Father we tend to project those rules on that relationship too. *And that will determine the nature of the relationship.*

Now I'm challenging you to (1) identify what you understand those rules to be, and (2) test them out biblically to see if they are God's terms of this ultimate relationship. I guarantee you his ways are different than yours and mine. As we emotionally and intellectually see the difference, we'll experience the most remarkable intimate relationship that exists.

FOR REFLECTION

It's important that you involve yourself in what you've read. Therefore, I'd like you to jot down your thoughts to the following:

1. Write what you understand to be the terms or conditions necessary to have an intimate relationship with God.

2. Where did you learn about the terms or conditions you've listed above?

3. Jot down specific Bible passages that you are aware of that describe those terms or conditions that you've listed.

4. What further questions or comments do you have about what you've read?

2.

GUILTY OF LIBEL

These earth dwellers! How hard it is to understand them.
They are so quick to believe the lies of the Evil One. And they
seem prone to doubt the eternal integrity of their all powerful
Sovereign. He never lies; he is the embodiment of Truth. Yet they
turn from him to the father of lies. How can this be?

Today I watched one of my Sovereign one's children stand and
listen to the blatant lies of the Evil One with an unquestioning
mind. He attends church every week but it doesn't seem to help
him. He didn't even use the Scripture he's memorized as a sword
against the lie. It puzzles me!

— Diary of a Puzzled Angel

DECEIVED!

Have you ever heard someone say "I'm dying for a smoke?"

In the 1940's and 1950's marketing cigarettes was big business. Advertisements touted smoking as a way to generate sex appeal, as a way to be a sophisticated person, as a pleasurable experience. One manufacturer even said that smoking was a way to guard against throat-scratch. [1]

A naïve, gullible public was deceived about the perils inherent in smoking. But what was even worst was we discovered that cigarettes were killing us. We now know that pregnant women who smoke increase the danger of birth defects in the unborn child. Smoking contributes to COPD, heart attacks, cancer, strokes, and emphysema.

As an easy to fool grade schooler I was almost caught. I attended a country school and during the noon recess my buddies and I would sneak into the woods and find our cache of cigarettes that we had hidden in a creek bank. We thought we were being macho having our smokes. I am thankful that it was a brief experience and I never became addicted. I could have easily been caught in the snare and suffered the consequences later in life.

Many such temptations surround us and how easy it is to be deceived about something with such innate dangers. Yet, in a world system under the influence of Satan many are seduced by perils that leave an indelible mark on their lives. In direct or indirect ways the Evil One seeks to trap individuals with his subtle promise of life, liberty and the pursuit of happiness.

Take Eve for example. God's first created woman.

One day Eve had a conversation that radically changed her life and the lives of all who would follow in her lineage. Hers is an account that should arouse passion in us as we enter into the event with Eve.

We read about it in the third chapter of the book of Genesis:

> Now the serpent was more crafty than any other
> beast of the field that the LORD God had made.
> He said to the woman, "Did God actually say,
> 'You shall not eat of any tree in the garden'?"
> And the woman said to the serpent, "We may
> eat of the fruit of the trees in the garden, but God
> said, 'You shall not eat of the fruit of the tree that
> is in the midst of the garden, neither shall you
> touch it, lest you die.' " But the serpent said to the
> woman, "You will not surely die. For God knows
> that when you eat of it your eyes will be opened,
> and you will be like God, knowing good and
> evil."
> Genesis 3:1-5

We believe that the serpent was a creature that the Devil was using to destroy all the beauty and peace that Adam and Eve were experiencing. Let's delve beneath the surface and explore what is happening in this incident. We can do this by asking ourselves several questions.

1. What kind of relationship did Adam and Eve have with the Lord prior this life changing event?

The first two chapters of Genesis don't give us the complete answer to this question. But we do know quite a bit about the Garden.

We know that it was a healthy environment. No cancer, heart attacks, asthma or salmonella. Adam and Eve didn't have to worry about smog and pollution. We know that the Lord of the Garden was kind, compassionate, warm and friendly. The

Garden was a safe place because he was Adam and Eve's protector. It was a place of *complete peace and abundant joy*.

We have enough data about our Lord to know that Adam and Eve experienced a level of intimacy with him that has not been known since. For example, we know that they were created with a sinless purity that allowed them to see God without distortion. And they shared his radiant beauty because they had been created in his image. They reflected God's beauty and grace in a manner that left them with a sense of oneness with him. They must have known that they were like him (Genesis 1:26) and this allowed them a basis for open, rich communion with him.

Then too, they were naked and not ashamed (Genesis 2:25). This unlimited transparency left no emotional barrier between Adam, Eve, and our Lord. Yes, they had a solid foundation for *unrestricted intimacy*. Both of them could approach him with innocence and transparency and share whatever was on his or her mind. No hesitancy, no fear, no barrier.

And, we have no record that the couple had any *worries or distractions* to interfere with this refreshing communion with God. They had a freedom and a mental clarity that allowed their minds to be uncluttered with pressures and problems that we face today. They were at peace with each other, the animals around them, and especially at peace with the One who had created them.

Chapters one and two of Genesis also leave me with the impression that Adam and Eve had *full access to their Lord*. He walked with them in the Garden. They could see him, talk to him, ask him questions. They could gaze upon the radiance of his smile and respond with unhindered joy. It is not unreasonable to believe that there was laughter and the richest of emotional and spiritual intimacy.

An enviable relationship!

But a life changing encounter with a serpent changed all that. And this leads us to a second question:

2. How did the serpent reshape Eve's view of God?

From the information Genesis gives us we believe that Eve had an open, innocent relationship with the Lord. She trusted what he said and what he did. This freedom allowed her to move about the garden unhindered. But a sinister plot was being hatched by the Evil One that would ruin the beauty of Eden.

One day the serpent engaged Eve in a conversation that would destroy the beauty of her innocence. Most important, it would forever change how she related to the one who had lovingly created her. She would never again enjoy the friendship and communion she had known with her Lord.

Our first information about this evil creature is that "the serpent was more crafty than any of the wild animals the Lord God had made" (Gen. 3:1). We need to pause here and clarify some information about the serpent. Unwise artists usually portray this scene with a snake coiled around a tree branch with Eve standing nearby. The Bible makes it clear that *this was not the snake that Eve encountered.* In verse 14, after the events we are examining now, the Lord places a curse on the serpent. The curse changed it into a creature that crawled on its belly as we see them today. So Eve must have been conversing with an upright creature that was intelligent. What she didn't realize was that she was encountering someone who could manipulate her mind and reshape her thinking. She didn't realize that she was in a dangerous and vulnerable position.

The serpent's attack was to subtly undermine Eve's belief in her Lord's integrity. He asks, "Did God actually say, 'You shall not eat of any tree in the Garden'?". After Eve answered his question the crafty one launched a bold attack to erode her confidence in her Lord's credibility. First, he challenged the Lord's statement that "of the tree of the knowledge of good and evil you shall not eat, for in the day that you eat of it you shall surely die."

But the crafty foe pressed even further. He directly attacked our Lord's integrity when he told Eve, "God knows that when you eat of it your eyes will be opened, and you will be like God, knowing good and evil" Gen. 3:5). The serpent's words implied that Eve's God was deceiving her and robbing her of the opportunity to experience life more fully.

In effect the serpent said, "Eve, you're a naive young woman. Read my lips. You can't trust your Lord. He's holding back from you because he doesn't want you to be on equal footing with him. He's looking out for himself. Eve, you'd be wise to look out for yourself and not be so dependent on him! Why be committed to someone who is robbing you of the full potential of your life."

Tragically Eve believed the serpent's lie!

If you read through the Bible you'll find that the serpent reveals Satan's first line of attack on us — he attacks the credibility of our Lord. He asks leading questions about God's motives. He sows the seed of doubt in our minds that our Lord isn't who he represents himself to be. He undermines our confidence that God is good, loving, and trustworthy. *Satan knows that if he can erode our confidence in our Lord the whole relationship with him is jeopardized and will falter or completely collapse.* Erode trust and you erode a relationship.

3. How did the serpent's manipulative words change Eve?

Eve might have thought that she was having a friendly chat on a sunny day. But the sly serpent had a determined, evil, deadly agenda. He intended to gain access to Eve's mind and twist her ideas, attitudes, and behavior. His attractive, winsome manner was a cover, allowing him to disarmed her so he could poison her mind without her realizing it. When he was finished Eve had become a radically different person. Her harmonious life was corrupted in at least four significant ways.

First, *the seeds of doubt were sown in her mind.* When the seeds of doubt are dropped in the soil of a person's thought life it is extremely difficult to root them out. When the words, "You can't trust God," are whispered in your ear the germ of suspicion is sown and will germinate into distrust. Because Eve was naïve she had no way beyond her Lord's words to reject the lie.

Second, *the serpent suggested an alternative way Eve could live her life* — seemingly a better way for her. Prior to this conversation Eve had no reason to question living under her Lord's loving care. Until now she had never thought about arguing with God, demanding her rights, or wanting equal billing with him. But the serpent whispers words in her ears that imply, "There are other options. Better options. You're foolish to let him run your life."

Third, *this new alternative opened the door for independence.* Eve is urged to do it her way, independent of the Lord. In fact, the serpent implies that since the Lord is hiding something from her Eve would be wise to launch out on her own and find truth for herself. Reaching for that attractive forbidden fruit was her declaration of independence. I can imagine the serpent affirming so warmly, "Atta girl. Go for it. Be your own person!"

Fourth, *the serpent challenges Eve to rebel against God.* No words can describe what a tragic, foolish act that was. But remember, we are seeing this incident after the fact, knowing what the consequences will be. Eve didn't have that luxury. Reaching for the alluring, but forbidden, fruit set in motion circumstances that would forever change the course of her life, her husband's life, and all people that would follow them. What seemed like a golden opportunity was history's darkest moment and greatest tragedy.

4. How has Satan reshaped our view of the Lord?

When we read about Eve's downfall we are apt to think, "What a stupid thing to do! Eve, you should have known better." But, we'd better be careful. If we think that we have immunity from the subtle seduction of the evil one we're very naive. It's clear from the Bible that Satan developed a master strategy to seduce people away from our Creator and into the evil one's diabolical control. And he intends to seduce us as much as he seduced Eve. If he can distort our understanding of God he will reshape our relationship with him.

The cunning tactics undertaken against Eve reveal the heart of the evil one's approach. What he did to Eve he has done to all of us.

WHAT WE KNOW ABOUT SATAN'S STRATEGY

Let's briefly review some of the characteristics of the evil one's strategy. First, We have already noted that this evil one is *incredibly clever*. We read in Genesis 3:1 that "the serpent was more crafty than any of the wild animals the Lord God had made." Second Corinthians 11:14 informs us that "Satan disguises himself as an angel of light." Anyone who thinks of the devil as a goofy, wild-eyed creature in a red suit with horns and a pitchfork believes an old fable. Our enemy cleverly presents himself as a warm, caring, thoughtful person.

Second, we learn that the evil one has a *well-planned strategy*. We are told that he has clever "schemes." There is not a chance that we will recognize how we are being seduced unless we are dressed in our Lord's full protective armor. That's the only hope we have to withstand his sneaky assault (see Ephesians 6:13 for more on this). The good news is that through this divine equipping we can become knowledgeable about his strategies and be less likely to be victimized by him.

Third, we know Satan is *single-mindedly persistent*. When the apostle Peter wrote his first letter to early Christians he warned his readers "Your adversary the devil prowls around like a roaring lion, seeking someone to devour." (1 Peter 5:8). Let's not think that we can resist him and he'll get bored and go away. Our enemy never gives up. If we don't fall for one of his tactics he'll come at us with another.

Lastly, we note that Satan's strategy is *powerful*. Paul makes this clear when he admonishes us that "For we do not wrestle against flesh and blood, but against the rulers, against the authorities, against the cosmic powers over this present darkness, against the spiritual forces of evil in the heavenly places" (Ephesians 6:12).

Occasionally I'll hear someone talk as though he is going to whip the devil with one arm tied behind his back. Such babbling is fool's talk. None of us are competent to contend with him in our own wisdom or strength.

THE FOCUS OF SATAN'S ATTACK

The most powerful attack Satan can make on us is to distort our view of God and to discredit our Lord's integrity. He lies to us about the conditions or terms of our relationship with our loving Father. And we believe him! *No matter how educated you are, or how long you have been a Christian you still have some ways that you have been deceived by the evil one concerning our Lord.*

If you don't face this fact then you'll be repeatedly exploited and blindsided by the evil one. He works his wily way in us in our early childhood before we are alert enough to understand what is happening. All of us have had our minds and emotions shaped from birth by the world in which we live. Parents, siblings, teachers, neighbors, media, and others have impacted us. Satan's whispers, lies and insinuations against God have influenced these people directly or indirectly. And we have believed much or all of it.

We're conscious of some ways we've been deceived, but don't know how to be freed from them because they're so deeply rooted in our mind and emotions. Some lies are hidden so secretly in our minds that we aren't even aware that they exist. (We can liken them to computer viruses that have been placed in our computer systems unawares to us and then at some unexpected moment create all sorts of problems). But the effect of conscious or unconscious misconceptions of our Lord robs us of intimacy and often leads us to discouragement, disappointment and denial.

SATAN'S BASIC STRATEGY

As we investigate this incident with Eve, we learn an essential life principle for ourselves. What we observe in this brief biblical incident teaches us something about the Evil One's basic strategy toward us. The most fundamental attack he makes on you and me is to corrupt our view of the God of heaven and earth—our heavenly Father. If he can create confusion, distortion and doubt in our minds and emotions concerning our Lord he will have corrupted the relationship. We are not in the Garden of Eden. We are not innocent. He may approach us through different channels and different circumstances but ultimately his goal will be the same.

• He may use an earthly father to corrupt our view of our heavenly Father.

• He may use an unbelieving teacher to mock our belief in the Bible.

• He may lead us to misinterpret a life circumstance to see our Lord as uncaring, insensitive or mean-spirited.

Because he is so clever, and knows us so well he has a whole bag of tricks that he can draw from. The point is he is committed to get us going down the wrong path, a path that is leading us away from a faithful, loving God who devotes himself to our security and blessing.

Pause for a few moments to reflect on your relationship with our Lord. What words would you choose to describe it? I've made four suggestions below that are meant to jog your mind about possibilities.

• You may be a person who is racked with guilt every time you pray, feeling that your heavenly Father hates you.

• You may feel as though he has abandoned you and is never there when you need him

• You may have difficulty praying; the Lord may seem distant, unapproachable.

• You may experience the Christian life as a routine without much personal meaning other than fulfilling the demands that others have told you God expects of his followers.

What is the nature of your Father/child relationship?

I hope that you find your heavenly Father to be the most wonderful, most awe-inspiring person you've ever known. I hope that you find him utterly trustworthy so that you rest peacefully in his loving arms moment by moment, day by day, every day of your life.

I have been relating to followers of Christ for over a half century and during that time I find a high percentage of Christians who have distorted views of their heavenly Father. When I interact with these people I find that the nature of the relationship with their Lord is lacking in intimacy, trust and fulfillment. Because Satan's fundamental strategy is to distort our view of our Lord we can be assured that all of us have some misunderstanding, confusion and warp in how we see him. Thus, the relationship is not what he would like it to be.

Let me offer a few examples that are based on real people. I've changed names and circumstances, but these illustrations are based on real situations Christians have encountered.

When you talk to Angie about God she bristles and says, "God is irresponsible! If he really cared he wouldn't let innocent people suffer." Even when Angie sees a dead animal at the side of the highway she blames God.

Bill is a crotchety senior citizen who grew up under "hellfire and brimstone" preaching. His parents were responsible about providing for his daily needs, but expressed little emotional warmth toward him. He was taught that the Lord didn't like Christians who danced or played cards. Bill tells me, "I've trusted Christ as my Savior, but I feel distant from him. If I play rummy at the Senior Citizens' Center I feel guilty."

Laura came to me for counsel about her interpersonal relationships. Her body language communicated a lot of anxiety. She nervously drummed her fingers on the arm of the sofa. As the conversation progressed I asked, "How would you feel if Jesus came and sat down beside you?" "I'd be very uncomfortable and I'd want to get up and leave," she replied. Laura had been sexually abused and feared men. To her God was a man.

I'd known Darren and his family for several years. He'd shared his struggles with me from time to time. One day as we were out for a morning walk he said, "You know, Norm, I feel as though I started climbing a ladder. But when I think I'm nearing the top rung I look up and see the ladder extends quite a bit further yet. Then I climb some more, only to realize the ladder never ends. I feel like I'm on an eternal ladder. Pleasing God is a never-ending ordeal. It's very depressing."

Do you see how this chapter connects to the earlier one? Satan is unswervingly committed to confusing you and me about the terms and conditions of a relationship with our loving Father. He tripped up Adam and Eve and ruined their lives. Don't think for a minute that you and I are immune from his diabolical plan. No, he has had many years to infiltrate our mind and emotions.

So our challenge is to open ourselves up to the Holy Spirit's searchlight. As we allow him to lead us to the truth about this amazing relationship he will root out the lies that rob us of the richness, joy and power of living moment by moment in our Father's presence.

FOR REFLECTION

1. Think of a time when someone deceived you in a way that made a significant impact on your life. How did the person do it? How did you feel after the deception?

2. What misconceptions of God our Father, or Jesus Christ have you heard? How have they undermined your relationship with the Lord?

3. What have you learned about Satan's strategy that will help you resist him?

4. If you could interview Jesus while he was on earth how do you think he would describe his relationship with his heavenly Father?

3.
FILTERS THAT SHAPE OUR PERCEPTION

The Eternal One is so patient! I don't think I could keep from getting angry at all the foolishness I've seen among his followers on earth. But I guess it's difficult to live among all that mental, moral, and spiritual pollution around them and not have it influence them. I just wish they would see more clearly our Sovereign's indescribable love, wisdom, and faithfulness. If only they'd consistently look to him. I wonder why they don't?

I can see that the Lord's children have been brainwashed with lies and half-truths. The Evil One has conditioned their minds to believe a lie and reject truth. Most of them have been schooled in lies and deceit from childhood. Even "spiritually mature" men and women don't see how they still are in bondage to subtle deceit.

How sad. It robs them of indescribable joy. Oh, that their minds would be transformed by the blessed Spirit.

— Diary of a Puzzled Angel

DISCOVERING A LIFE CHANGING PRINCIPLE

"The mind can only see what it is prepared to see."[1]

Most of my adult years have been an adventure of trying to make sense of my relationship with my heavenly Father. Subconsciously, whenever I read a book, listen to a recording, watch a movie, or interact with someone else I'm listening for some insight or truth that will expand my understanding of this all-important relationship. It's a positive hunger to intimately know my compassionate, powerful, and loving Father. I feel like the apostle Paul as he spoke about his own passion to know God. He said, "Indeed, I count everything as loss because of the surpassing worth of knowing Christ Jesus my Lord." (Philippians. 3:8).

During one of these receptive moments I was reading the book *Principle-Centered Leadership*. The author, Stephen Covey, made a statement that reached out and grabbed my attention:

> I've found that if you want to make slow, incre-
> mental improvement, change your attitude or
> behavior. But if you want to improve in major
> ways — I mean dramatic, revolutionary, trans-
> forming ways — if you want to make quantum
> improvements, either as an individual or as an
> organization, change your frame of reference. . .
> change your *paradigm*.[2]

My mind went on "red alert." I recognized that what Covey was saying was insightful and was challenged to give this my undivided attention. After all, I knew that the Christian life is to be a transforming experience. I recalled verses that said:

- "Truly, truly, I say to you, unless one is born again he cannot see the kingdom of God" (John 3:3).
- "Be transformed by the renewal of your mind" (Rom. 12:2).
- "And we all, with unveiled face, beholding the glory of the Lord, are being transformed into the same image from one degree of glory to another" (2 Corinthians. 3:18).

Covey's statement reminds us that some growth occurs if we work on attitudes and actions. I find that a sobering reminder because too often we are trying to reform attitudes or change behaviors to be a better Christian when our Lord is whispering to us, "You're missing the point. It's about transformation, not reformation! You mean well, but you're going about it the wrong way."

So Covey's words launched me on a pursuit to better understand what paradigms are all about. And I wanted to see how paradigms related to my hunger for greater intimacy with my beloved Father. So I began to ask myself a series of questions. The first was . . .

WHAT ARE PARADIGMS?

The word *paradigm* comes from the Greek word *paradigma*. It is a word that describes how we comprehend the reality that is around us.

Think of paradigms as grids through which we make sense of life. Or, as rules or instructions that govern how we function. Or, think of paradigms as mental structures that help us solve the multitude of problems and tasks that we face daily.

It might even help you to think of them like the contact lenses a person wears to "see" the world and make sense of it. Without lenses everything is a blur.

For many years I wore glasses with lenses like the bottom of Coke bottles. I learned to experience my world through the distortion that the lenses created. I thought that I was seeing things as they really were. Then my doctor friend told me that I could have cataract surgery. In the process the lenses in my eyes were removed and new ones were inserted that made my "coke bottle" glasses unnecessary. I was experiencing the world in a new way. I felt an exhilaration knowing that I would never need to look at the world through distorted lenses. I've experienced a freedom that has changed my life.

Paradigms, whether correct or distorted, help us make sense of life. We do this instinctively. Otherwise life would be too complicated.. We make decisions about how to respond in certain situations without conscious thought. Think, for example, of how naturally and thoughtlessly you drive your car. You know the proper sequence of what to do and how to do it. You know that you have to insert the ignition key first. You know just how much pressure to apply to the accelerator pedal so the engine doesn't run too fast. If your car has a manual transmission you know that you have to depress the clutch before shifting the transmission. And you know which gears have to be used in sequence.

In the process of assimilating and integrating vast amounts of information related to driving an automobile, your mind has cleverly formed a mental concept — a paradigm--of what it means to operate a vehicle. You do it with little or no conscious thought because you have a perception of what is entailed and you can undertake the task automatically. Somewhere in the hidden labyrinths of your mind you're told what to do, when to do it, and how to do it. And the beauty of it is that your conscious mind is left free to do other things like carry on a conversation with your passenger! That's the power of paradigms.

WHY ARE PARADIGMS IMPORTANT?

Our most important paradigms focus on two areas: the way we perceive things to be (what is real), and the way we perceive how things ought to be (what's important or valued). Recently, I've been in touch with three people who are involved in an emotionally packed dilemma. Each person's paradigm is telling them what is real (to them) and what is important (to them). In private conversations with each individual I've been keenly aware that each person sees the situation and the circumstances surrounding it through different lenses — his or her own unique perspective. What one person sees as an opportunity the other sees as a threat. What prompts sadness in one prompts anger in another. They are viewing the same situation — the same reality. But their personal paradigms cause them to perceive and respond to this event in completely different ways.

And their paradigms are shaping their relationship with each other. At this point I'm a bit nervous because I recognize that a faulty paradigm of reality can ruin their relationship.

Even scientists who pride themselves with objectivity are influenced by their paradigms. Thomas Kuhn, a scientific researcher speaks of this as he describes how paradigms relate to the scientific community. As he watched different scientists at work he noted that "practicing in different worlds, the two groups of scientists see different things when they look from the same point in the same direction . . . they see different things and they see them in different relations one to another. That is why a law that cannot even be demonstrated to one group of scientists may seem intuitively obvious to another."[3] Kuhn's insight is significant. He recognized that highly trained scientists who were committed to objectivity still had internal mental structures which determined what data they saw and how they interpreted it.

No matter how intelligent or well-educated we are, we all live by, and make choices by, our paradigms — those grids screen information and tell us how to make sense of it.

WHY DOES IT MATTER WHICH PARADIGM I HOLD?

When I was a boy a watch was made from springs, gears, and hands. But in 1967, a Swiss research group came up with the concept of the quartz crystal watch. Presto, no more springs, gears and hands! But when it was displayed at a trade show the Swiss manufacturers expressed little interest in this new invention. To them a watch was springs, gears, and hands. But representatives from Texas Instrument and Seiko saw something different when they saw the new Swiss prototype. They saw a paradigm shift. So these two companies began to make quartz crystal watches.

Prior to World War 2 the Swiss watchmakers claimed about 90% of the market. But the early 1980's left them with only 10%. In fact, their workforce was reduced from 65,000 to 15,000 employees in the brief span of 1979 to 1982. The way the general population perceived watches had changed and the Swiss lost the market. They failed to recognize an important paradigm shift.[4]

Many other examples of far-reaching changes could be mentioned.

For example, in 1876 a twenty-nine-year-old inventor named Alexander Graham Bell received a patent for the telephone. In 1877 he offered that patent to Western Union for $100,000. They rejected the offer believing that the telegraph would be the preferred means of communication. Yet today the telephone industry has annual revenue in excess of $200 billion. And the telegraph key is a collector's item.[5]

Actually telephones have gone through a series of paradigm shifts. In the early years people listened in on a party line that connected phones in the neighborhood. Then a shift occurred in which a person could have a private line. Now most people are not tied to a land line, but carry a cell phone with them wherever they go. This has required new behaviors in which we are told to turn off our cell phones so they will not distract those around them. Cell phones have created a new culture of communication through texting. Laws have been passed to restrict the use of phones in automobiles.

But let's be honest. Most of us resist paradigm shifts because they change the rules of how we operate and that leaves us feeling uncomfortable. (How many people refuse to stop talking or texting on their phones while driving?) Most of us prefer the comfort and security of the way things have always been done. In fact, our paradigms become so much a part of us that we don't realize how they've "colored" our thinking. I use that word deliberately because it reminds me of my sunglasses. As a resident of Arizona with its superabundance of sunshine I keep my sunglasses nearby. I have at least four pairs. One pair is very dark so when I put them on my world looks comfortably dimmed. The glare is gone. But I also have a pair that has yellow lenses. When I slip these on my world looks bright and cheerful—even on a cloudy day.

After I've had my sunglasses on for a while I forget about them and begin to assume that I'm seeing my world as it is. But the truth is my sunglasses have changed my perception. With one pair the brights are filtered out, with the other the brights are enhanced. My paradigm—my sunglasses—has altered the real world, but I forget that fact and assume I'm seeing it as it is.

You must be able to see by now that paradigms are powerful constructs that guide the way we think, the way we perceive our world, and how we understand what is real. Whether we want to acknowledge it or not all of us use paradigms like I use my sunglasses, but we don't realize how much they shape our thinking and influence the choices we make. Our paradigms shape how we experience life and relationships. They are essential to make sense of life and allow us to live efficiently. They give direction and set boundaries for our lives and thus they are important inner mental organizers. But because they operate quietly, out of view, we rely on them without questioning their accuracy.

So in one sense paradigms are good. But they also have a negative side. If our paradigms are partially or totally defective, our minds will block or distort data that could lead us to freedom and joy. It makes sense to reevaluate how accurate our perceptions are.

When a person changes a paradigm, it unleashes the potential for radical life change — genuine transformation. Like the apostle Paul at his conversion experience, the scales fall off our eyes and we have new vision (Acts 9:1-18). We will never be the same again. The person who envisions a new paradigm is able to "think outside the box," and perceive a reality outside the established boundaries--like the Swiss research team who found a new way to measure and record time. This brings things into a new light. As the Bible says, "the old is gone, the new has come" (2 Cor. 5:17). The old is now obsolete..

New paradigms can be very threatening to the person who has become comfortable with the established order. A new way of perceiving the world disrupts their security and lifestyle. And those who have a vested interest in the old way will likely resist the new because it may put them out of business. They may lose their status and control. They may be looked upon as a "has been." That can be very disconcerting.

WHAT DO PARADIGMS HAVE TO DO WITH GOD?

At this point you may be thinking, "This talk about paradigms is interesting, but I don't see what it has to do with my spiritual life. What's your point?" That's a good question! In answering it let me ask you some questions?

• When did you form your understandings about yourself and God?

• How did you form these understandings?

• How do you know that your paradigm is accurate? (How do you know that your spiritual sunglasses don't have tinted lenses?)

• How do you know that your understanding of the terms and conditions of this relationship are correct?

Let me propose a good natured bet! I'll bet that you have never seriously considered where you got your understanding of God and whether it is consistent with what the Bible teaches. And the odds are in my favor that you have some distortions that are robbing you of the full joy and freedom that our Lord intends for you to experience.

Consider the following quote: "The research tells us and clinical experience bears it out, that people in their thirties and forties made their decision about the worthwhileness of life most often somewhere in the fifth grade."[6] Many of our paradigms were formed in childhood. In fact, I'm certain that the mental structures that have shaped how we perceive our God and how he relates to us were formed during our childhood years and through relationships that were not related to him. As we formed our sense of how significant relationships work we simply transferred them to this relationship. And we did it subconsciously so we never realized the filters or grids that were shaping the way we perceived the relationship.

One of the fascinating things about the Bible is that it is almost constantly describing paradigms and paradigm shifts. Here's a sampling:

• The Bible is divided into the Old and New Testaments. Under the Old Testament framework, people understood that their relationship with the Lord was based on keeping the Law. In the New Testament a new paradigm is presented. Now we are invited to a relationship based on our Lord's grace expressed through the death of Jesus Christ on our behalf. Moving from the Old Testament paradigm to the New Testament is genuinely life changing.

• The Jews who had been deeply schooled in the Old Testament found it extremely difficult to move away from it's orientation to the freedom Christ offered in the New Testament. It had become so deeply rooted in their thoughts and feelings that it was hard to change.

• Jesus said that "Whoever finds his life will lose it, and whoever loses his life for my sake will find it." (Matt. 10:39). What a radical thought!

• Later he said, "unless you turn and become like children, you will never enter the kingdom of heaven" (18:3). How do adults become children? What did he mean?

• He also said that we are to "bless those who curse you" (Luke 6:28).

• The apostle Paul stated that "Therefore, if anyone is in Christ, he is a new creation. The old has passed away; behold, the new has come." (2 Corinthians 5:17). He gives us a new way of seeing ourselves.

• Our Lord said to Paul, "My grace is sufficient for you, for my power is made perfect in weakness" (II Cor.12:9). Do you hear the paradigm shift? How can power be exhibited in weakness? How can we make sense of Paul's joyous response, "When I am weak, then I am strong" (12:10). It only makes sense if we recognize that we are now being given a new perspective through which to understand life.

I cite these examples to help you see how our Lord consistently challenges the way we've learned to think about ourselves, our lives, and our relationship with him. The Bible is so radical! How difficult it is to understand if we keep looking at it through our old lenses — our old paradigm. It's equally disastrous to consider that we may bend God's truth to make it fit our perception of what we think is real.

But now let me ask you a crucial question.

HOW ARE OLD PARADIGMS LIMITING MY RELATIONSHIP WITH GOD?

The Scribes and Pharisees were deeply religious men. But they were rooted in old paradigm thinking. They were highly educated in the Old Testament Scriptures. They kept the Law and sacrifices with incredible diligence. Yet when Jesus came in the power of the Spirit, with a message of redemption and promise they soundly rejected him to the point of plotting his death. How could such a thing be? Why would individuals turn away from someone who extended a valid offer of forgiveness from their sins and an eternity with their Lord?

It is not difficult to see if you realize that everything Jesus said threatened their well-polished thoughts and their well-crafted religious ideas. Like the Swiss watchmakers, they rejected the new and held tightly to the old. They spurned the golden opportunity and chose the security of familiar but false reality. They were interpreting his every word and action through an old paradigm of what they thought was real. But their faulty lenses cost them dearly. Rather than opening their arms to him with love and excitement many of them became dedicated adversaries. It's sobering to realize that even the apostle Paul once saw Christians as adversaries to be killed until he had a profound paradigm shift and saw a new life-changing reality.

But let's move beyond the Pharisees to our own lives. What filters keep us from knowing this warm, gracious Father as he really is? What has conditioned us to limit the potential fullness of this relationship?

To some extent all of us have a distorted perspective when it comes to knowing him as he really is. One reason is that we tend to view him through the relationship we've had — or lacked — with our earthly father. If he was harsh or inaccessible we tend to see our eternal Father in the same light. I might memorize Scripture that tells us he's accessible but struggle to enjoy my relationship with him emotionally because my current belief system won't acknowledge the truth.

Another reason we've gained an inaccurate perspective is because we live in an imperfect and confused world system. Most of us have been affected by confused messages that have influenced our thinking — sometimes without even knowing it. J. B. Phillips wrote a book entitled *Your God Is Too Small*. His point was that we have learned to see our Lord in inadequate and distorted ways that rob us of his strength, warmth, and intimacy. It's apparent that our Enemy uses the same tactics on us that he did with Eve. He works hard to distort our view of our heavenly Father. He strives to discredit our Father's love and integrity toward us. We've been misled and don't recognize how it's impacting this precious relationship.

WHICH WILL IT BE? MY PARADIGM, OR GOD'S?

Our tendency is to fit our Lord into our paradigm rather than allow him to show us his. A person's natural response to new truth is to assimilate it into existing data. That works well for some things but is dangerous when it comes to spiritual truth. In Isaiah 55:8-9 our Lord himself addresses this. Listen to his words:

> For my thoughts are not your thoughts, neither
> are your ways my ways, declares the LORD. For
> as the heavens are higher than the earth, so are
> my ways higher than your ways and my thoughts
> than your thoughts.

Until we recognize that our heavenly Father's reality — his paradigm — is radically different from ours we will continue to manipulate, squeeze, and force him to fit our preconceived reality. That's a natural response. He requires us to lay our paradigms aside and come with a humble, teachable spirit and let him bring us into his paradigm of reality. That is true biblical transformation.

I'd like to share with you the story of Steve, a Christian who was trapped in a faulty paradigm:

> I lived many years of my Christian life trapped
> in what I call the motivation-condemnation-
> rededication cycle. From the earliest years of
> my Christian life, I had a mental picture of what

I thought I should be. In this picture there was always a wide gap between where I ought to be and where I was. Sometimes when I was especially motivated, I would feel that the gap had narrowed a bit. When I was winning people to Christ or, spending a lot of time praying and studying the Bible, I felt that I might actually one day be able to bridge the gap and be a victorious Christian.

But inevitably, my motivation level would diminish and my fury and fire would die down. That decline always led to a sense of condemnation. Even when I had done nothing wrong. I would feel guilty for not doing all the things that I believed I should be doing. The devil had a field day with me during this phase. Sometimes I would become spiritually indifferent. Other times I would wonder if I would ever be consistent in my Christian life.[7]

That's the challenge before us. That's why I challenge you to reevaluate what you've always believed were the terms and conditions of an intimate relationship with your heavenly Father.

FOR REFLECTION

1. Who has shaped your view of your heavenly Father ?
How did they shape it?

2. What life experiences have influenced how you perceive
your heavenly Father?

3. Do you think that you have an accurate, biblical understanding of who your heavenly Father is and how he wants to
relate to you? Why or why not?

4.
IS YOUR "GOOD NEWS" REALLY GOOD NEWS?

Why is it so hard to believe that a free gift is really free? Why do the shepherds put stumbling blocks in front of those they lead? It baffles me why they say, "God's gift of salvation is free, but you'd better prove to the Lord that you are worthy of it. Prove it by your good works. The Lord loves those who work hardest."

If I were the Holy One I'd be upset when the shepherds imply that I need some return on my investment to be appeased. The Holy One is fully sufficient in himself and doesn't need someone to prop up his ego. He gives good gifts because he is good. He finds delight in those who receive the gift of eternal life as a bona fide unrestricted gift from his gracious heart.

Oh that they would learn.

— Diary of a Puzzled Angel

IS THE GOSPEL REALLY "GOOD NEWS?"

The phone rings, and when I pick it up I hear a warm, cheery voice greeting me as though I'm the caller's best friend Immediately my "Be careful" sensor lights up with a red alert! The caller says something like . . .

"Mr. Wakefield. Or can I call you Norm? I'm calling to tell you that you are the lucky recipient of a very valuable prize. It's absolutely free. Norm, we've got a one-week trip to the Bahamas for you and a guest. Could we come by your house and deliver this wonderful prize? What night could we come by when you and your wife would be home?"

You know the rest of the story. The "free gift" is actually a decoy to get me to sign up for some expensive timeshare that involves thousands of dollars. It's not a free gift. It's a clever trick to enslave me with financial debt. The "gift" is a gimmick.

I remember my first experience in the "free gift" sales approach. Winnie and I were newlyweds living on a shoestring budget. Our neighbor, Jim, invited us for a "free" dinner that would be cooked by a person who sold stainless steel cookware. We didn't want to offend our neighbor so we accepted the invitation. First, we listened to a short spiel about the product and all the ways it would revolutionize cooking. Next came the supper. Then the sales person made appointments with each guest within the next week. That ended the evening.

As the time approached for our appointment I began to feel anxious. I knew that the man intended to make a sales pitch and the product — though excellent — was well beyond our budget. When we tried to explain to him that we didn't have the financial resources to make such an investment he became indignant. Needless to say, I didn't enjoy the experience. So our "free meal" did cost us something.

WHEN IS "FREE" FREE?

We live in a media-driven culture with an overwhelming number of messages bombarding us daily. Many try to convince us that we need what they're selling. It seems we cannot live a contented life unless we have the product or service that's being offered. We're promised extraordinary features, greater comfort, better relationships with others, and so on. Sometimes we hear that the product is free. Or we'll get a "free" gift for signing up.

The very idea of a gift suggests that it is free. No strings attached. The dictionary says that a gift is "something given voluntarily and without compensation; a present."[1] It's certainly true that some individuals say that they are giving a gift, but have ulterior motives for giving it. Thus it's not a gift. A spoken or unspoken message exists, "I expect something in return."

I said earlier that the terms and conditions of a relationship determine the nature of that relationship. Our understanding of the gospel, the "good news" about our relationship with our beloved Lord, is crucial. What you believe about the gospel will shape this relationship more profoundly than anything else. It is the bedrock issue that a person has to settle to understand the basis for this eternal relationship. What do I mean?

One of the controversies among earnest Christians today is whether our Lord's gift of eternal life is truly free. Many say the gift is free, but then add qualifications. "God's gift is free, but . . .," or, "You can become a child of God if . . ." and then other requirements are added. My impression is that many of us find it hard to believe that our Lord would give us a gift without any strings attached. We can't accept that all we do is take the gift and enjoy it.

In one sense it's good that this struggle exists. It shows that we're aware of how helpless and hopeless we are, and how

evil and misguided our actions are. It ought to make us gasp
to think that the eternal Lord, our Creator would offer us an
unconditional pardon and invite us into the intimacy of heaven
itself with full standing as family members. It's not bad to find
ourselves thinking, "That's unbelievable. No one would do such
a thing. I can't comprehend such a thing." But we need to let
our Lord be the ultimate authority, and if he says that his love is
unconditional then it's unconditional.

WHAT IS GOD'S "GOOD NEWS"?

The biblical word "gospel" means "good news."

In 1 Corinthians 15 the apostle Paul says to his readers,
"Now I would remind you, brothers, of the gospel I preached
to you" (15:1). Then he proceeds to outline what the good news
consisted of. "For what I received I passed on to you as of
first importance; that Christ died for our sins according to the
Scriptures, that he was buried, that he was raised on the third
day according to the Scriptures, and that he appeared to Peter,
and then to the Twelve" (15:3-5). Paul's definition of the gospel
holds important insights for us.

Paul tells us that the gospel is about Jesus Christ. It is about what
he did on our behalf. He died. He was buried. He was raised.
He appeared. The good news is about what Jesus Christ did; *it is
not about what I do.* The good news is only about me in the sense
that it is applied to my condition. I was lost and in need of help
beyond my own ability. Jesus Christ stepped in and addressed
that need by his and our Father's initiative. Now he offers his
work on my behalf as a gift to me.

*Paul also describes how this good news is integrated into my
life.* First, Jesus Christ acts on our behalf — died for our sins,
was buried, was raised the third day. Second, this message is

communicated to us so I hear it and receive it as my Lord's gift to me. Third, I internalize it so that I now stand on the truth (verse 1) of what was done on my behalf.

The good news is that which I believe was done on my behalf. I am called to make that the basis for my relationship with my beloved, heavenly Father.

The best known verse in the Bible is John 3:16. It was spoken by Jesus one evening when an inquiring Pharisee, Nicodemus, sought spiritual help from him. What many don't know is that just prior to uttering those words Jesus gave his night visitor a picture from the Old Testament that vividly describes the simplicity of the good news. Jesus told Nicodemus, "And as Moses lifted up the serpent in the wilderness, so must the Son of Man be lifted up, that whoever believes in him may have eternal life" (John 3:14-15).

The incident Jesus referred to is recorded in Numbers 21:4-9. The children of Israel complained against God and Moses. They allowed sin to harbor in their hearts. Finally our Lord brought punishment on them in the form of poisonous snakes that bit the people. Many died. Then they hurried to Moses and asked him to pray that God would remove the snakes. So Moses prayed. Our Lord gave Moses the following instructions: "Make a fiery serpent and set it on a pole, and everyone who is bitten, when he sees it, shall live." So Moses complied with the Lord's directions. An infected person who looked on the bronze serpent on the pole lived.

This is an amazing incident.

Wicked people who deserve to die are granted life by merely looking at a bronze snake on a pole. All a person had to do was look at the snake. No matter how evil their actions had been, if they believed that looking on the serpent would save them they were saved.

Jesus takes this Old Testament incident and says to Nicodemus, "*Just as* Moses lifted up the snake in the desert, *so the Son of Man* must be lifted up, that everyone who believes in him may have eternal life" (Italics added). Just as looking on the serpent brought life to dying Israelites so looking at Jesus Christ bearing my sin in his body on the cross and believing that he is my Savior imparts eternal life to me.

If you've been taught a false view of our Lord's good news then you'll have a difficult time believing that a relationship with our heavenly Father and Jesus Christ can be based on such a simple action. But these are not my words, they are the words of Jesus Christ, God's beloved son. The gospel is not about my promises to my Lord of how good I will be. It is about looking, by faith, to Jesus Christ and seeing that he paid the penalty for my sins. Our Lord says, "Look to Jesus Christ. Believe that he took your place on the cross. Put your faith in his work and you will receive the gift of eternal life."

When our Lord gives a gift it really is free!

PAUL'S GOOD NEWS

The early years of my Christian life were characterized by much uncertainty about the terms and conditions of my relationships with my heavenly Father. I'd confessed Jesus Christ as my Savior and endeavored to be a diligent Christian, but I found ample reason to believe that my Lord might want to kick me out of the family. But gradually, as I grew in the knowledge of the Word of God, I began to see that a consistent theme ran through Paul's writings that left no doubt concerning the good news about my relationship with Jesus Christ and my Father.

A few years ago I decided to make careful note of what Paul had said. Because of limited space here I want to put before you just a few of the clear convictions of what Paul knew about the free gift our Lord has given us.

Listen to what he said (with my italics added):

> The righteousness of God *through faith in Jesus Christ* for all who believe.
> (Rom.3:22)

> For all have sinned and fall short of the glory of God, and are justified *by his grace as a gift,* through the redemption that is in Christ Jesus.
> (Rom. 3:23, 24)

> For we hold that one is *justified by faith apart from works* of the law.
> (Rom 3:28)

> For while we were still weak, at the right time *Christ died for the ungodly.*
> (Rom. 5:6)

> *While we were still sinners,* Christ died for us.
> (Rom 5:8)

> *While we were enemies* we were reconciled to God by the death of his Son.
> (Rom. 5:10)

> And you *He made alive,* who were dead in trespasses and sins.
> (Eph. 2:1)

But God, being rich in mercy, because of the great
love with which he loved us, even when we were
dead in our trespasses, made us alive together
with Christ—*by grace you have been saved.*
(Eph 2:4, 5)

And you, who were dead in your trespasses
and the uncircumcision of your flesh, *God made
alive together with him*, having forgiven us all our
trespasses."
(Col. 2:13)

As I read through these verses and many others, three consistent truths stood out to me. First, there is a consistent emphasis on our Lord's initiative. The good news is about what he did,
not what I did. The gospel is about an indescribable love that exists in the bosom of our Lord that prompted him to provide the
free gift of salvation to us. Second, I notice a consistent emphasis
on our lostness. We were helpless, sinners, dead, and enemies. I
had nothing to offer him that would appeal to him in any way.
Isaiah reminds us that "all our righteous acts are like filthy rags"
(64:6). When we realize that we were spiritually dead we can
grasp that *we have nothing to contribute* in our coming to God.
The third consistent emphasis I saw was that we were made
alive totally by our Lord's initiative. That's why our relationship
with our Lord has to come as his free gift to us. We have nothing
to contribute.

What you believe about the gospel has a major effect on the
kind of relationship you will experience with your heavenly
Father. If he invites you into a relationship that is totally his
loving gift to you then you will experience an open, joyous

relationship. Your gratitude to your Father and our Lord Jesus will soar. But if you understand the gospel as something your heavenly Father gave to you with conditional strings attached then you will experience a different kind of relationship. You will be forever conscious of whether you're "measuring up," whether he is looking at you with displeasure, whether he is withholding his love because you didn't perform properly, and so on. That's why I say that this is the first issue you must settle in your mind or heart.

What I have written here is very personal to me. For too many years my relationship with my heavenly Father was shaped by my feeling that I had to perform for him to receive his love. When I began to see that his love was never conditioned on my behavior a transformation occurred in my life. It didn't cause me to become careless and indifferent about my relationship with my Lord. Rather it had the opposite effect. I found myself irresistibly drawn to such an indescribably lovely Father.

I want the same for you.

FOR REFLECTION

1. Have you ever been offered a "gift" with strings attached? How did you feel knowing that you had certain obligations to fulfill? Did you enjoy the "gift" as much as you would have if it had been given with no conditions?

2. What difference does it make in your relationship with your heavenly Father if your salvation is an unconditionally free gift from his loving heart, or if it is something he offers you with certain conditions?

3. Read Ephesians 2:8, 9. Do these verses suggest that our Lord's gift has conditional strings attached? Why do you answer as you do?

4. Is receiving a gift with no strings attached more likely to make us sin? (than if conditions are attached?)

5.
TWO WAYS TO PASS THE COURSE

Today I listened to a child of the Sovereign One confess her sins. She begged and pleaded with her heavenly Father to forgive her many wrongdoings. She listed them, went over the list again and again, . When she was done she felt fear and anxiety that her Lord was going to hold them over her head when she got to heaven. She says that she believes the Bible, yet acts as though what it says isn't true. After all, the Sovereign One has said, "Their sins I will remember against them no longer."

The blessed Son, Christ Jesus, took the penalty for this woman's sin when he died on that horrid cross. When she received the Holy One's gift of eternal life she received forgiveness. It's that simple. Why does she allow her day to be ruined by thoughts and feelings of false guilt.

I'm confused. Why doesn't she believe the words of Holy Scripture?

— Diary of a Puzzled Angel

LET'S MAKE A DEAL

For many years I've been a seminary professor. During that time I've discovered that most graduate students are very grade conscious. When the semester begins they want to know what the terms and conditions of the class are. What are the course requirements? When are assignments due? How many pages does the research paper have to be? Usually these questions are posed because the student wants to be assured of a certain grade.

At the beginning of the semester I tell my students that I won't give them the course requirements until about three weeks have passed. I want them to determine what they want to get out of the class apart from the issue of grades. This announcement immediately creates anxiety among some who get nervous when they don't know what the expectations will be. So on about the fourth class session I hand out an information sheet that outlines the course requirements. You can read them it yourself.

CD501 Course Grading

To receive an "A" in this course you will need to:

1. Read and accurately memorize both textbooks.
2. Each week you will be given a two-hour take home exam. It must be typed, grammatically correct, with no spelling errors. You will be responsible to have complete knowledge of the reading assignments and anything the professor has said in class the previous weeks
3. You are to write a 100 page term paper following the exact procedures outlined in Turabian, *A Manual for Writers of Term Papers, Theses, and Dissertations.*

4. You must memorize every verse in the Psalms which refers to God. In addition, you will submit a 50-page paper on "The Theology of God in the Psalms." You will need to defend your paper before the entire seminary faculty.

5. No absences are allowed and you must be in class ten minutes prior to class time.

To receive a "B" in this course you will need to:

1. Read and accurately memorize both textbooks.

2. Each week you will be given a two-hour, take-home exam. It must be typed, grammatically correct, with no spelling errors. You will be responsible to have complete knowledge of the reading assignments and anything the professor has said in class the previous weeks.

3. You are to write a 95-page term paper following the exact procedures outlined in Turabian, *A Manual for Writers of Term Papers, Theses, and Dissertations.*

4. You must memorize every verse in the Psalms which refers to God. In addition, you will submit a 45 page paper on "The Theology of God in the Psalms." You will need to defend your paper before the entire seminary faculty.

5. No absences are allowed and you must be in class ten minutes prior to class time.

It is fascinating to watch and listen to the students' responses! Usually there's a lot of laughter that indicates that they know that I couldn't be serious about expecting such a high standard of accomplishment. After all, a person would have to be a "perfect" student to achieve it. But then I ask my students what their thoughts and feelings would be if these course requirements were genuine. By now I'm prepared to hear remarks such as:

"I'd want to drop the course."

"I'd feel that to try would be hopeless."

"I'd get angry feeling 'This isn't fair.'"

Students understand perfectly the predicament they are in.

- they are not "acceptable" unless they meet my standard of perfection.

- it's an impossible standard for them to achieve.

- to try is an exercise in futility.

But the learning exercise isn't over yet. Having established a standard of perfection that the students can't hope to achieve, I tell them. "Okay. I'll make you a deal. Imagine that there is a student — we'll call her Robin-- who can achieve this standard of perfection without breaking a sweat. Whenever Robin reads something it is locked in the brain forever with instant and perfect recall. Robin can make an "A" because she does everything perfectly. So here's my deal. If you want to identify yourself with Robin I'll give you a grade based on what she has done. I'll accept her work on your behalf. All you have to do is tell me, "Prof, I'm with Robin. Credit her work to me." (I jokingly tell my students that at the next class students would be crowded around Robin and saying to me, "Remember, Robin's work counts on my behalf.")

I'll guarantee you that by now I have my students' undivided attention. I want them to "see" a profound truth about our relationship with our beloved heavenly Father. If you opened a theology book to find this truth it would be called *justification*.

JUSTIFICATION: WHAT IS IT?

The Bible clearly states that "None is righteous, no, not one; no one understands; no one seeks for God." (Romans 3:10,

11), and, "all have sinned and fall short of the glory of God" (Romans 3:23). These statements tell us that we are hopelessly lost apart from some gracious act by our Lord. He is perfect; we are flawed. He is pure; we are impure. He is holy; we are sinners. His essence is radiant with glory which powerfully reveals our hopelessness. To hope, wish or delude ourselves into thinking that we could measure up to this standard of perfection is foolishness. Our dilemma is clearly outlined in the Bible.

Our Lord knew our hopeless condition. He knew that we were lost. Though he loved us with a perfect love he still couldn't shut his eyes to our sinful, rebellious state and act as though nothing had happened. He wanted to reach out and invite us into his presence, but he couldn't do that without addressing our sin in a just manner. So he sought a way to justify us.

Justification is the means by which a righteous God with an uncompromising standard of perfection is able to unconditionally accept sinners into his family. Justification has to do with the basis by which my loving Father can accept me into a warm, intimate, personal relationship with himself. When we are justified the penalty of any sin or failure is removed as a barrier to the relationship. Now an unhindered two-way relationship can take place between our Lord and us. We can communicate openly and freely.

Justification is not something done in me, but something declared of me. When I am justified by the work of Jesus Christ on my behalf our heavenly Father says that I am righteous. The day we bowed our head and claimed the work of Christ on our behalf we were announced as righteous, but we did not stop sinning, or gain the ability to live a perfect life

Andy has been incarcerated at a state penitentiary. He was found guilty of robbing a bank. But a judge has pardoned him and declares that he is free to leave prison. Andy still has the same strengths and weaknesses. The habits and personality that he had prior to his being pardoned haven't vanished. Yet a legal proclamation has been given changing his status in reference to the offense.

Justification has to do with my standing before my heavenly Father. Prior to this pronouncement I was unacceptable, an outcast and under a severe penalty. But when the declaration is given, my standing changes to a fully vested son in the family with all rights and privileges that others have. I can come boldly into his presence without fear of scorn, ridicule, or rejection. The writer of Hebrews tells us "For we do not have a high priest who is unable to sympathize with our weaknesses, but one who in every respect has been tempted as we are, yet without sin. 1 Let us then with confidence draw near to the throne of grace, that we may receive mercy and find grace to help in time of need." (Heb. 4.15, 16)

I can see his loving face inviting me to come near and enjoy his company.

Justification settles two issues related to my relationship with my Father: My Father's standard of perfection, and my sins.

First, it addresses the issue of my inability to live up to my Father's perfection. Remember the illustration I gave you of my standard of perfection that I held before my students. They felt hopeless to meet my expectations. They were powerless to accomplish what I was asking of them. No matter how many late nights they poured over the books and how much they agonized trying to memorize enormous quantities of information they would always know that they would fail.

But I gave then another option. As a pure gift of grace I let them take the work of another and I said I'd credit it to their account. All they had to do was take me up on my grace-filled offer. As ludicrous as it sounded I would be legally binding my-self to accept another's work in place of their failure. It would be a bonafide offer.

Romans 3:10-31 is a clear, powerful, and profound statement of our being justified by a loving Father. Verse 10 says in the clearest, most pointed language that "there is no one righteous, not even one." Apart from our Lord's gracious action we were hopelessly lost with no power to measure up to the righteous standard a holy God had every right to require.

Paul stresses that no matter how diligently we adhere to the Law it still wouldn't accomplish this feat. He says in verse 20: "For by works of the law no human being will be justified in his sight, since through the law comes knowledge of sin."

Rather than making us feel better it leaves us sickeningly aware of how far short we are coming. Then...

HOPE WHEN ALL SEEMS HOPELESS

...just when we have lost all hope of experiencing intimacy with this holy God, Paul reveals an astounding truth:

"But now the righteousness of God has been manifested apart from the law, although the Law and the Prophets bear witness to it — the righteousness of God through faith in Jesus Christ for all who believe." (verses 21, 22).

Be sure to catch these points:

• Our Lord provides a righteousness from another source than ourselves. He identifies it as a righteousness from God himself. He puts his righteousness in place of our flawed, in-fected righteousness.

• This new God-given righteousness is apart from the Law. In other words, it is not our trying to achieve a standard of holy life by obeying rules, but his holy life given as a gift.

- This righteousness comes through Jesus Christ. We know that he is the righteous Son of God. At the cross he took the punishment we deserved and our heavenly Father substituted Jesus' righteousness in place of our sin. Remember how students could take Robin's work on their behalf? This human illustration points to a true and majestic reality of one who took my failure and put in its place his perfection. It was granted as a pure gift to those who would accept it.

- Romans 3:27 makes it clear that this new standing is apart from our effort. "Where then is boasting? It is excluded." I will never see my relationship with my beloved Father as something that I've brought about by anything that I've done. I come freely into his presence because of what another has done on my behalf.

- If you read through Romans 3 you will notice that "righteousness" is mentioned six times, "justification" is mentioned six times, and "faith" is mentioned seven times. Righteousness and justification always come through faith in what Jesus Christ did on our behalf. I am justified by believing what was done by another on my behalf.

BUT WHAT ABOUT MY SINS?

So what does this mean to our relationship with our Father? After all, in myself I am spiritually bankrupt. But a loving heavenly Father credits Christ's perfection to my account.

When he looks at me he sees Christ and his perfection — his righteousness. Because of this he extends an unconditional welcome to come and enjoy his friendship — purely as a loving gift! Because of this gift you and I have a solid basis whereby we can see our Father's smiling face beaming at us and his arms extended welcoming us into his presence.

I said earlier that justification tackles two issues. We have considered the first one-- how our Lord dealt with the problem of our lack of righteousness. But a question remains "How can my sins be forgiven?" Just as he can't wink at my lack of perfection he can't ignore my sin.

Because he is a righteous God whatever he does must be done righteously. Somehow the problem of our sins must be resolved without compromising truth. Thankfully the Word of God addresses the issue of our sin with clarity.

Paul addresses the problem of our sins in his letter to the Romans. Consider the following verses:

"For while we were still weak, at the right time Christ died for the ungodly. (Rom. 5:6)

"Since, therefore, we have now been justified by his blood, much more shall we be saved by him from the wrath of God. For if while we were enemies we were reconciled to God by the death of his Son, much more, now that we are reconciled, shall we be saved by his life.!" (Rom. 5:9, 10).

These passages describe how our Lord dealt with the problem of our sins when Jesus Christ bore them on the cross in our place. Theologians speak of the substitutionary death of Christ on the behalf of sinners. What they are saying is that he took the penalty we deserved so we do not have to bear its consequences. Our wise, loving heavenly Father created a just way that he could forgive us of our sin.

A series of Old Testament passages makes it clear that our Lord is eager to forgive us and is dedicated to provide a way that it could be accomplished.

In Psalm 32:1-2, David says "Blessed is the one whose transgression is forgiven, *whose sin is covered*. Blessed is the man against whom the LORD counts no iniquity, and in whose spirit there is no deceit" (italics added).

Notice that David recognized that a provision could be made so that a person's sins could be covered. We know that Jesus Christ covered our sins at the cross so our Father doesn't count them against the individual who receives Christ's punishment on his behalf. In a later Psalm, David says that *"as far as the east is from the west,* so far does he remove our transgressions from us."* (103:12 - italics added). It's impossible for the east and west to ever meet. In like manner one whose sins have been forgiven will never face them again.

Isaiah also affirms the finality of our Lord's forgiveness. He says to the Lord, "But in love you have delivered my life from the pit of destruction, for you have cast all my sins *behind your back."* (38:17 - italics added). Can you visualize what he's saying? Whenever we put something behind our back we cannot see it. It's another way of expressing that the sin is put away with finality. A few chapters later the Lord himself speaks and says, "I, I am he who blots out your transgressions *for my own sake,* and I will not remember your sins." (43:25 - italics added).

This is an amazing revelation of the heart of our Lord. I see three insights that give heartfelt encouragement.

• Our Lord blots out our sins. What is blotted is gone. It doesn't exist any more.

• Our Lord does this for his own sake. I was overwhelmed when this truth hit me. I always felt great gratitude that he would remove the penalty I deserved. But I finally realized that my heavenly Father himself wants the barrier of sin removed from our relationships. It finally occurred to me that he values his relationship with his children so much that he sought forgiveness so he could love us freely. In a sense he did it for himself as well as for us.

• Our Lord says that he will remember our sins no more. Think of this. The sins that you and I have committed are no longer in our Lord's mind. He has chosen to remember them no longer. I used to think that when I got to heaven my Lord would spend the first number of years scolding me for all the sins I had committed. When I read this verse for the first time I experienced the liberating joy that such was not his intentions at all. The penalty for those sins was paid for by another so Father will never hold them to my account again. Even now I must say "Hallelujah!"

The prophet Micah gives us a final insight on how eager our Lord is to put the issue of sins away. "He will again have compassion on us; he will tread our iniquities under foot. You will cast all our sins into the depths of the sea." (7:19). In Micah's day anything hurled into the depths of the sea was permanently gone. His word picture is example of the enthusiasm our Lord exhibits to forgive us and see an intimate relationship restored.

Since our Lord is so diligent to tell us how he has cleared all the roadblocks for an open, loving, intimate relationship it's a shame that many of his children fail to maximize this grand opportunity. He holds the door open to us to come freely into his presence to enjoy unhindered fellowship with him.

HOW SHALL WE THEN LIVE?

From our study it is clear that our loving Father has done an indescribable act to nurture a warm, positive relationship with us. He has graciously wiped away the barriers that kept us from an intimate relationship. He has redefined the terms and conditions of a relationship with him. He can do no more.

Do I recognize the profound invitation that he extends? Am I ready to let go of unhealthy, unbiblical ideas and attitudes that keep me from receiving his friendship, guidance and love? His arms of invitation are extended.

FOR REFLECTION

1. A friend comes to you and asks, "What does it mean to be 'justified?'" Write out your response in as clear and simple a way as you can that is accurate biblically.

2. Why was it so critical that our Lord make a way that we could be justified?

3. What does the truth of justification have to do with having an intimate relationship with our Lord?

4. Are you absolutely certain that you are justified in your heavenly Father's sight? On what evidence do you base your answer?

5. Are you absolutely certain that your sins — past, present and future have been fully paid for by Jesus Christ on the cross?

6. In what way is a person's life different when he is absolutely certain that he is justified as a free gift from a loving heavenly Father?

6.
HOW MUCH IS A PENNY WORTH?

This has been a super day! I had such joy seeing John's spiritual eyes open to the wonderful truth that the Sovereign One cherishes him dearly. He had been so depressed believing the lie that he was a worm in his heavenly Father's eyes. A part of the problem was that he'd been trained to believe a lie. Other Christians kept telling him how unrighteous he was in the Holy One's eyes. They seem to forget that the Holy Scriptures say that their heavenly Father has credited Jesus Christ's righteousness to those who come to him.

The Sovereign One's truth is so liberating, so life changing. It excites me to see one of his children see the glorious reality. If only all of his followers would believe what he says.

— Diary of a Puzzled Angel

HOW A PENNY CAN BE WORTH A DOLLAR

I've gained a reputation among my friends as a lover of cartoons. Cartoons intrigue me because they remind us of our hang-ups, habits, or prejudices. We chuckle because the cartoonist captures our inconsistencies and we can't help but laugh. I have one before me that takes place in a sports arena. The first, second, and third place winners are at the dais with the respective athletes standing on each side of the first place position — which is elevated two feet higher. A lad who's about seven years old is trying to climb up to the first-place position while the men look on in embarrassment. The cartoonist is reminding us of those situations in which someone younger or with less experience excels us and we are left feeling foolish.

Perhaps one reason I grimace when I see this cartoon is because I have zilch athletic ability. My height of achievement was running a 10 K race and finishing about 100 out of 125 entrants. I remember huffing and puffing for what seemed like eternity until finally staggering across the finish line. And I had trained for it! Yes, I am genuinely intimidated when pressured or cajoled to join any competitive sports event. I run and hide, feeling as though I will be a liability to my team and face their scorn when I goof up.

I discovered my athletic value when I was a grade-schooler. When baseball teams were chosen in the neighborhood I was always chosen last and my team demanded special concessions from the other team because they got me. It didn't take me long to decide on my worth.

All of us long to succeed in something that gives a feeling of importance and value. We want a sense of achievement. We want to accomplish something that others see as significant. Some of us are endowed with natural abilities that make achievement come relatively easy. Others have to work hard to reach the same level of competency. And then there are others that achieve and are affirmed for it but still experience that nagging feeling that they are insignificant and not worth anything. They feel worthless.

PERSONAL WORTH: I NEED IT

Words like self-esteem, significance, and worth are popular buzz words today. Speakers and writers remind us that self-worth is essential for mental and emotional health. Psychologists and educators emphasize how crucial it is that a person feels good about himself. The ability to function successfully in life is generally tied to the way we see ourselves.

So how does an individual come to feel valued? How does that person feel significant about who he is and what he is able to achieve? And for those of us who are followers of Jesus Christ, the most important question is "Does my heavenly Father value me?" We want to know if God provides some way that we can value ourselves and what the Bible say about this.

First, let's clear the deck and say that *the idea of self-worth is really a fallacy.* "Self-worth" suggests that there is some way that I can look at myself and come up with an objective way of placing a value on who I am. But that is an impossibility because *worth is always formed in reference to others.*

Let me illustrate.

If you have some coins, put them where you can look at them. The basic four consist of a penny, a nickel, a dime, and a quarter. The value of each coin is determined by its relationship with the others. Some unknown person in the past decided that a nickel would be worth five times the value of a penny. A quarter got to have twenty five times the value of the lowly penny.

By now you may be thinking, "Well, the quarter is bigger than the penny." But I'd remind you that the dime is smaller that the penny yet is given a value ten times greater. Why?

We may try to rationalize the value of items but usually someone else has placed a value on them and we come to believe that they are really worth more. The same principle applies in relationships. We value some individuals because we decide that they are "worth more" to us than others.

We value people because:
- they have more money.
- they come from a certain ethnic heritage.
- they are more physically beautiful.
- they have outstanding mental abilities.
- they have great physical prowess.
- they live in a certain section of town.
- they practice an esteemed profession.
- they exhibit certain character qualities.
- they come from a prestigious family line.
- they have a winsome personality.

The list could go on endlessly because we have an uncanny ability to set value on certain assets, circumstances or qualities and rank individuals according to that criterion.

When I think of this I am reminded of Harvey Weinstein, a New York millionaire and chairman of West Mill Clothes Co. In the summer of 1993 Fermin Rodriguez, a sewing-machine operator who worked for Weinstein, kidnapped him and held him for a 3 million dollar ransom. His family paid this huge sum of money because they valued Harvey. To them he was worth 3 million dollars.[1]

Could you imagine Harvey Weinstein's family saying to his kidnappers, "We've talked it over and agree that he's not worth that kind of money. We'll give you twenty five dollars for him.

Otherwise keep him and we'll keep the money!" How would Harvey feel? Whether they paid the ransom or not would be a tangible indication of what they thought he was worth.

Now put yourself in this same situation. What would your family pay for you? Would they scrape up the 3 million? Or would they say to your captors, "He/she's not worth that much. Keep him/her!"

Second, *our sense of worth is established by those around us.* As you grew up you didn't determine your worth, it was those people around you that kept communicating what you were worth in their eyes.

A woman was talking to a friend about the influence a mother has on her children and her friend. As they were talking, the friend told about her childhood experience. She explained that when she was a small child, her mother would hold her in her arms and starting with her toes, her mother would say:

"I love your little toes,
I love your little feet,
I love your little ankles,
I love your little legs,
I love your little thighs . . ."

Then she would work her way up the child's body and lovingly say, "I love your little neck, chin, mouth, nose, eyes, ears, face, hair . . ."

She continued,

"I love you when you're good,
I love you when you're bad,
I love you when you're clean,
I love you when you're dirty."

So powerful were the mother's words that when she was twelve years old she would still find herself crawling in her mother lap to her those loving affirmations.

This incident demonstrates the powerful effect of her mother's loving words and actions in communicating how precious her child was to her. We can also vividly see what this valuing did in shaping her sense of worth. This example points us to the source of our personal worth. Other significant people keep telling us what we are worth by their words and actions. Some of us have received consistent positive affirmation of our worth to them. Some of us have received a mixture of positive and negative strokes. And some have received largely negative indicators that say, "You're worthless."

Think of these people as mirrors that reflect to you an image of yourself. The image reflected by them leads you to believe that what you see in their comments, attitudes, and behaviors is who you are. If the "mirror" shows you a positive reflection then you come to believe and feel warm and content. But if the "mirror" image is someone who is a nuisance, bad, foolish, ugly, and so on, you will believe the image is really you and not feel good about yourself. It is also crucial to remember that the image is not merely a mental image. Perhaps even more important it is an emotional feeling that brings you joy or pain.

THREE WAYS WE FORM OUR SENSE OF WORTH

As I've pondered this issue I see that we form a sense of worth in three ways. The first two will always ultimately be disappointing, but the last — which is our heavenly Father's unique way of establishing worth can be life-changing.

The first is what I call *imagined worth*. It's largely based on fantasy and has no real substance. Carlos imagines he is a great ballplayer with the crowds cheering him because of his amazing ability to hit home runs. At best he is a mediocre ballplayer, but he never lets himself face the truth and lives with the illusion that he is someone that he really isn't. Jackie also lives with imagined worth. She envisions herself as a beauty queen that everyone else adores when in truth she is average in appearance. She dresses and acts in a way to maintain this illusion. She deceives herself because she wants to believe that she is of great worth.

Imagined worth may also express itself in the opposite manner. A valued team member may imagine that he is useless to the team, contributing nothing to its success. I have this tendency because I imagine myself as a liability to any team. If someone drags me onto the volleyball court I feel as though the team would rather I wasn't there. I see myself as contributing nothing of value. In my eyes I'm worthless to the team even though my participation may be as significant as other team members.

The second kind of worth is *inherent worth*. Inherent worth is the worth we place on someone because of some innate capacity, ability or skill that the person has. Usually this is a God-given ability or talent that the individual may or may not have, strengthened by training or personal discipline. Unfortunately we seem to have the knack for communicating greater worth to individuals who excel in some spectacular way and ignore or demean someone who has excellent character qualities or is faithful in fulfilling ordinary duties. A baseball team may have an outstanding pitcher who receives abundant adulation, but eight other players are just as essential to the success of the team. An outfielder may be a solid, contributing team member, but may not be seen as having the inherent worth that the pitcher does.

My son, Joel, had the opportunity to work as an intern one summer at a major league football training facility. He observed that some players saw themselves as God's gift to the team. These men were arrogant, self-centered, and cocky. Other team members were warm, friendly, and affirming of other players and staff. The first group felt that their inherent worth gave them rights and privileges not given to others.

We discover the natural tendency to see certain individuals as having more inherent value in a biblical incident found in 1 Samuel. The prophet Samuel was sent to the home of Jesse to anoint the next king of Israel. As he entered the house he observed Jesse's oldest son, Eliab. No doubt he was strong and striking because the prophet thought to himself, "Surely the Lord's anointed is before Him" (1 Sam. 16:6 NASB).

But the Lord cautioned him and said, "Do not look on his appearance or on the height of his stature, because I have rejected him. For the LORD sees not as man sees: man looks on the outward appearance, but the LORD looks on the heart" (verse 7). Though a godly man, Samuel gave worth to external form rather than the inner worth.

But there is a third kind of worth that I call *imputed worth*. Imputed worth is not based on any inherent quality within the individual, but in a value placed on the person by someone else. When we "impute" something we credit it to a person's account. I have illustrated this many times with an ordinary penny.

Imagine that you and I were chatting and during the conversation I offered to buy a penny from you for a dollar. At first you look at me to see if I'm joking, or crazy, and then you take a penny from your pocket. You glance at it and notice that it is a tarnished 1984 one-cent piece. Someone has rubbed the edge on the sidewalk so it's scratched. It doesn't look like a bargain. But I cheerfully hand you a crisp, new dollar bill and the transaction has been made.

HOW MUCH IS THE PENNY WORTH?

Your instinctive response is "One cent," and in one sense you are correct. But how much is that penny worth to me? One dollar. Because that's what I paid for it and I now give it a value beyond its inherent worth. The tarnish and scratches don't matter because I didn't purchase it because it was beautiful or in mint condition. It's worth to me is credited on the basis of what I paid for it. The Bible calls this imputed worth

Now imagine that another person hears of our transaction and says to me. "I'd like to buy that penny. I'll pay you $500,000 for it' (And you thought I was crazy to give you a dollar for it!) So he gives me a cashier's check for $500,000 and I give him the penny.

NOW, WHAT'S THE PENNY WORTH?

Well, in terms of U.S. monetary value we could still say one cent. But in terms of what another was willing to pay for it it's worth a half million dollars. The person who paid that huge price wouldn't consider the penny as worthless because he had paid a great price for it. The owner would likely say, "I'd like to show you my $500,000 penny." And people would line up to look at it. Newspaper articles would be written about it. Writers would interview the owner to try and understand what would possess a person to make such an astounding transaction. I wouldn't be surprised if that plain, tarnished 1984 penny ended up in the Smithsonian Institution.

No one would be able to understand what prompted a person to make such an incredible purchase. It defies human logic so it would have to be based on some totally different source of motivation—a motivation we can't grasp. But the fact that the transaction took place couldn't be denied.

WHAT ARE YOU WORTH TO YOUR FATHER?

I'm guessing that about now you are saying, "Norm, that's a stupid illustration. No one would pay such a ridiculous price for something with so little inherent value. But hold on, because my illustration has a parallel far greater that you can imagine. In fact, all that's been written thus far in this chapter prepares us to face an even more incredible truth than the $500,000 penny.

Someone paid a price for you and me that makes my illustration look trivial in comparison. Someone said that your worth was beyond human comprehension.

When the apostle Paul outlined our Lord's mind-boggling plan to redeem you and me he demonstrated very clearly how precious we were to our Lord. I've long marveled at his words to the Romans that describe this. In the last chapter I examined the nature and scope of our Father's love and described how far reaching it was.

You may remember that he loved us:

• when we were weak and helpless. (Romans 5.6)
• when we were sinners missing the mark. (Romans 5.8)
• when we were his enemies, antagonistic to his purposes. (Romans 5.10)

Let's look at this in terms of our worth to God. Just as he loved us under the above circumstances he also credited worth by saying "You are worth the life of my beloved Son. You were worth the life of my Son:

• when you were weak and had nothing to offer me.
• when you were a sinner violating those things I cherish.
• when you were an enemy opposing my purposes.

Let my miracle penny be a faint picture of this stunning truth. The astounding price was paid totally apart from any inherent worth. The purchased penny was no better than any other. It was chosen purely from some desire to give undeserved worth to a penny. It's a picture of you and me. Our eternal Father loves us in a way that we will never be able to fully grasp.

As an act of pure grace he says "You are worth the life of my beloved Son." And he pays that gigantic price to weak, lost, helpless, sinning enemies.

He was not impressed by any inherent qualities of character or holiness. He credited/ imputed the highest measure of worth as a pure gift from a loving heart.

It's one of those indescribable aspects of our heavenly Father that we will never be able to comprehend.

What response could we anticipate in the life of those who know they are worth so much to our Lord? Even as Paul describes this profound valuing love he suggests what impact it will have on those who grasp its reality.

1. We enjoy a relationship of peace with our Lord (Romans 5:1). This one who values us so highly is at peace with us.

2. We enjoy a relationship rooted in grace. "We have obtained our introduction by faith in this grace in which we stand." (Romans 5: 2)

3. We experience joy because we have a thrilling future with this one who values us so much (Romans 5: 2).

4. We can endure hardship with a spirit of joy because one who cherishes us so much must have a high purpose for the trials he asks us to endure (Romans 5: 3). He is committed to bring out the highest measure of maturity and beauty that can be accomplished. I understand that problems and hardships have infinite value.

5. We experience a constant overflowing love from this one who values us so highly. (Romans 5: 5).

A PERSONAL PERSPECTIVE

Nearly 40 years ago, Annette Joy entered Winnie's and my life. Little did we know that day that our daughter possessed handicaps that would limit her cognitive abilities. Things that our other four children could do with ease Annette has never been able to do. Yet we valued Annette as much as each of the other four children. And the more we cherished her the more she seemed to blossom into a happy, friendly, loving person. Her beauty has exceeded what we could have anticipated. Her warmth, patience, and skill with children is exceptional. She has far more friendships with adults than most people. And what she has taught us about letting go of the unimportant things is a priceless gift. In the eyes of the world Annette may seem less mature, sophisticated, educated. But in the eyes of those who know and love her she has chosen those things that can never be taken away.

I've learned an invaluable lesson from our Lord when he sent Annette into my life. I see clearly that when we graciously credit worth to an individual it allows that person to thrive and become beautiful in spirit. That's what our loving heavenly Father accomplishes in our lives. When we are honest about our lost, hopeless condition it staggers us to know that our Lord would place such a high value on us. When we accept this fact by faith it transforms us in a profound way.

FOR REFLECTION

1. Think about your past life. What persons or circumstances shaped your sense of personal worth?

2. Can you think of people you know who build their sense of worth on inherent strengths or qualities?

3. How does it make you feel to know that your heavenly Father has generously credited worth to you? Why not write a prayer expressing your gratitude for this breathtaking act of love.

7.
INCREASING MY CAPACITY TO TRUST

Oh, how hard it is for the Holy One's children to trust him. They trust in their bank account, their insurance policies, their logical reasoning, an so on., but not the Trustworthy One, their heavenly Father. Too often his promises are ignored or rationalized so that they mean little or nothing to his children. Yet, the apostle Paul said, "He who calls you is faithful; he will surely do it." And the writer of Hebrews clearly said,"Let us hold fast the confession of our hope without wavering, for he who promised is faithful."

Yes, I affirm that the Holy One always keeps his promises. It is impossible for him to be unfaithful to his children. The Holy One is utterly trustworthy. I wish there was way I could get them to believe this truth every day, in every situation.

— Diary of a Puzzled Angel

WHAT'S MY PARADIGM OF GOD?

One of the main themes of this book is that we have been conditioned through a variety of life circumstances to view life through our own unique filters. We have been grappling with how our minds organize information into efficient ways of thinking so it is readily available. We call these packages of organized data paradigms. And one of the important "packages" of information and concepts is our understanding of our Lord.

For example, many Christians have packaged their relationship with him to include such ideas as:

- he expects me to perform to gain his acceptance.
- he has laid down impossible rules that govern my acceptance and whether he likes me or not.
- who I am is based on how others see me and how I stack up in relationship to them.
- when my Lord looks at me he doesn't like what he sees and is telling me that I'd better shape up.
- he expects me to read my Bible every day, obey without error, tithe my income, witness to everyone around me, etc. in order to be on his good side.
- he is disinterested in me, having too many more important things to care for.

When the paradigm of our relationship with our Lord contains these kinds of thoughts and feelings we can never develop genuine intimacy with him. There may be occasional "highs" when we think we are doing pretty well, but performance-based thinking always leaves us with the feeling that we haven't achieved what we should. And even if a person thinks he or she is an A+ Christian the nature of the relationship is falsely based.

The Spirit of God is endeavoring to lead us into a new way of thinking.

That's what we have been investigating so far. His new paradigm contains thoughts and feelings rooted in truths such as:

- my relationship with my Lord is rooted in his gracious love for me which never has to be earned.
- he has covered me with Christ's righteousness and counts that righteousness as mine.
- he says that who I am is not rooted in my earthly family identity, my social environment or my achievements, but I am a full-fledged member of his family with all the rights and privileges. All has been given as a free gift.
- my past, present and future sins were dealt with when Jesus Christ died on the cross. He says that my sins will be remembered against me no longer

I could keep adding to the list but the important thing for us to see is the difference between the two lists.

The first list puts the pressure on me to perform in such a way as to gain my Lord's acceptance and approval. The second list reveals that my relationship with him is based on my believing that what he has done for me is true.

The second set of statements that define my relationship with this wonderful Person has to be taken by faith. We believe that this is true because our Lord said it, not because we have scientific evidence. My faith that "what he says is true" becomes the crucial issue in defining and enjoying a relationship with our awesome heavenly Father and his Son, our Lord Jesus Christ. For that reason it is important for us to think through what we know about faith and how our life circumstances have influenced us to be skeptical or trusting.

LET'S PLAY THE TRUST GAME

Imagine that I ask you to stand facing the wall and I'm standing five feet behind you. You can't see me, but you know that I'm behind you. I ask you to fall backwards and I'll catch you. Will you do it? My guess is that you won't. One reason is that you don't know me well enough to trust me. You don't have enough information about me to risk falling. The other reason is that you don't know whether I'm capable of catching you. You might trust my integrity, but you can't trust my ability.

So you don't know me or my ability to catch you. But is there someone that you'd let stand behind you and catch you? It's possible that you might not trust anyone. And perhaps even if Jesus Christ was inviting you to fall into his arms you'd resist.

This simple activity tells us something about our trust level.

HOW DID I LEARN TO TRUST—OR DID I?

We can ask ourselves "How does a person learn to trust?" Does it happen automatically? Or do certain life experiences shape my commitment to trust others, or to be a skeptic trusting no one.

Years ago a developmental psychologist by the name of Erik Erikson taught that each of us goes through a series of developmental stages as we pass through life.[1] Each stage has a defining issue that has to be settled. The way we settle the issue builds the foundation for the next stage. Erikson said that the first stage which occurs from birth until about eighteen months of age is the issue of trust vs. mistrust. Instinctively the infant begins to sense, "Is the world in which I've been born trustworthy? Can I trust the people who are caring for me?"

As the youngster interacts with his environment he is seeking to determine the answer to that question. What he decides will influence his relationships with others, his fulfillment in life, and how he chooses to live.

So our early impressions from those around us shape our decision to trust others. The way a youngster is held can communicate a sense of security or a sense of uncertainty. The child senses nervousness, anger, calmness, peace, security, and so on. I've marveled at how different preschoolers are in their relationships with adults. I've noticed that some are fearful of strangers and hide behind their parents while others are inquisitive, friendly, and secure. Each is learning to trust or mistrust others.

As we grow we are influenced by significant people around us. I know a lawyer who grew up in a home where parents took him to church and Sunday school and he was taught to believe the Bible, taught about a heavenly Father and Jesus Christ. But when he got into law school at a state university he was barraged with cynical statements from his professors indicating that a mature person did not believe such "myths." The daily undermining of his faith in God, the Bible, and the church left him with substantial doubts about what he had been taught. I could see in the way he lived life and interacted with others that he had decided to trust himself and no one else, including God.

The words, attitudes, and actions of those we interact with affirm or undermine our decision to trust what we have been taught. Somewhere deep within us we formulate our convictions about the reliability of those around us and the truth about spiritual realities. Yet, most individuals don't stop to think about what has shaped their faith and consequently they are not get challenged to think through the basis of their belief.

Another influence that shapes our ability to trust our Lord is the extent of our biblical knowledge. In Romans we are told "But how are they to call on him in whom they have not believed? And how are they to believe in him of whom they have never heard? How are they to hear without someone preaching?" (Rom. 9:14, 15). Then Paul says, "So faith comes from hearing, and hearing through the word of Christ" (9:17). Someone has said that people today have knowledge about God that is a mile wide and a quarter-inch deep. It is difficult to place significant confidence in someone we don't know well.

It may be helpful to think of the sequence that leads to faith. First, I have to have knowledge of truth. Then I have to choose to believe that it really is true. And finally I must decide to place my faith in that truth and make it experientially mine.

A third shaping influence is the scientific mindset of our age which works against a healthy belief in God. The skepticism that says, "Only what can be seen, felt, tasted, measured, or tested in a lab is true," leads people to think that a settled confidence in the unseen is outdated or naïve. Such skepticism was evident in Jesus day, leading him to say, "Unless you see signs and wonders you will not believe" (John 4:48). And the postmodern thinking that all truth is relative also has shaped many people's mindset.

WHY TRUST IS CRUCIAL

Trust is crucial for any significant, healthy relationship. Ask yourself, "Do I have any meaningful relationship with someone I don't trust?" How can we draw close to someone that is

unreliable, deceitful or undependable? Alan Sieler, a profession-
al coach, says that "Trust enables relationships to develop and
flourish. Trust is the 'glue' that holds relationships together."[2] In
fact, can you ever really know a person you don't trust, or who
doesn't trust you?

Some of you who are reading this have grown up in dys-
functional families. You know about empty promises, deceit,
threats, and so on. You knew that you couldn't trust those
around you. You never told them about your disappointments,
your dreams, your uncertainties because you knew that they
would scoff, belittle, or ignore you. You knew that you couldn't
depend on what family members told you. You learned to live
in an untrusting environment. And you found it to be a disappointing experience. Inwardly you longed for something more,
but knew that it would never be realized within your family.

Lack of trust also makes it difficult, if not impossible, to
submit to others. We find it very hard to come under the instruc-
tion, leadership, or influence of those we don't trust. We feel
insecure and frightened to place ourselves under someone who
is not trustworthy. Consequently, we'll resist, argue, procras-
tinate, or give lip service as a means of protecting ourselves. I
have noticed that a significant number of women shudder when
the word "submission" is mentioned because their experience
with the word has been oppressive, demeaning, and controlling. It's hard to submit to one who exhibits these attitudes and
behaviors.

I have a friend, Kurt, who is a lawyer. He told me of a client
who was 89 years old and felt that he was near death. But after
knowing Kurt for only six months he gained a solid trust in him.
In fact, Kurt said that his client literally put his life in his hands,
allowing him to oversee his finances, choose his housing, and select his health care. As Kurt reflected on this unique relationship

he said that the man came to trust him because Kurt exhibited a gentle, loving concern, carefully listened to his requests for such things as putting together the man's will. Somehow in my friend's perceptive listening and his communication of a loving spirit the man felt he could trust Kurt and thus he submitted to his influence.

The Word of God makes it clear that we cannot have a meaningful relationship with our Lord without faith. We must come to the place where we can entrust our lives to his loving care, and where we believe what he has said and promised is absolutely true. The writer of Hebrews states this concisely: "Without faith it is impossible to please him [God], for whoever would draw near to God must believe that he exists and that he rewards those who seek him. (Heb. 11:6).

Trust also removes performance as the basis of our relationship with our heavenly Father. As Paul writes to the Romans he speaks of the intimate relationship Abraham had with his Lord. Paul says:

> If Abraham was justified by works, he has something to boast about, but not before God. For what does the Scripture say? "Abraham believed God, and it was counted to him as righteousness." Now to the one who works, his wages are not counted as a gift but as his due. And to the one who does not work but trusts him who justifies the ungodly, his faith is counted as righteousness
> (Rom. 4:2-5).

This is a beautiful and encouraging insight that Paul gives us. Our Lord is looking for individuals who will trust who he is and what he says. He is not asking us to appease him by a life of performance to gain acceptance. Rather, he is seeking men and women who will take him seriously and trust that what he says is truth. Their lives will then be lived in response to his faithfulness, not their effort.

One of the great men of faith in the modern history was George Mueller. On one occasion Mueller was crossing the Atlantic going to Quebec. He had an appointment there the following Saturday. The problem was the ship had encountered a dense fog requiring the captain to remain on the bridge for twenty-four hours without a break. He informed Mueller that it wouldn't be possible to arrive in Quebec by Saturday. Mueller replied, "Very well. If the ship cannot take me, God will find some other way. I have never broken an engagement for fifty-seven years. Let us do down to the chartroom and pray."

The captain felt Mueller was completely irrational and said, "Do you know how dense the fog is?"

Mueller replied, "No, my eye is not on the density of the fog, but on the living God who controls every circumstance of my life." Then this man of faith knelt and in simple terms placed his need before his Lord.

When he arose he said to the captain, "Captain, I have known my Lord for fifty-seven years, and there has never been a single day that I have failed to get an audience with the King. Get up and open the door, and you will find that the fog is gone." When the captain opened the door the fog was gone and Mueller kept his appointment.[3]

This account sounds rather dramatic, but it exhibits a godly man's deep-seated confidence that our loving heavenly Father is a person who keeps his word. George Mueller lived his life testing out the promises of his Lord and found that what he promised he fulfilled.

This deep, settled confidence in the living God is a power-ful adhesive that binds the child of God to his faithful, loving Father. There is something about the trusting heart that endears our Lord to his child. He delights to see us believe that he means what he says.

WHAT IS BIBLICAL FAITH?

Sometimes we hear individuals talk about faith as though it is something that is magically generated within a person. We are challenged to pray for faith as though it will be like a cloud descending from heaven, enveloping us in its mist. But a more biblical view is expressed by Larry Richards.

> The Bible uses "faith" in ways that link it with
> what is assuredly and certainly true. Christians
> may sometimes speak of "believing", as if it
> were merely a subjective effort, as if our faith
> or strength of faith were the issue. But the Bible
> shifts our attention from subjective experience
> and centers it on the object of our faith—God
> Himself.[4]

The root of faith is not something we drum up ourselves, but the result of our consistent act of gazing upon our Lord and finding a growing amazement of who he really is. As our knowl-edge and view of him expands, faith then grows within us.

Experiential faith is rooted in the facts that I know and the underlying emotions and attitudes that I have developed over the years. For my faith to grow I need to gain clear biblical facts, as well as clarify and refine any unhealthy emotions or attitudes that have worked their way into my life. A person who has grown up in a skeptical, unbelieving home may have developed a root of cynicism that interprets the Bible critically and judgmentally. A child who lived with adults who made repeated promises and never honored them will likely tend to discredit what others say as empty words without substance. Even when biblical facts are present the cynicism reinterprets the truth to satisfy the cynical spirit within the person.

It may be helpful for you to think of biblical faith in this way: *Faith is my decision to believe what the Bible says about the Lord – his personality, character, ability, promises – and the commitment to live by these truths.*

Faith then is built upon biblical truth. As I study the Bible and discover abundant statements about our Lord's integrity, love, power, and so on. I make a choice to believe that these statements are true. And I choose to align my thinking with what the Bible tells me. As my faith in my Lord and his truth grows I have a foundation to challenge lies and distorted facts. And I have a way to challenge my deeply rooted unhealthy or distorted attitudes. As this process deepens I find my growing faith produces a restful lifestyle, my life has a focused hope, and an infectious joy makes life fulfilling.

WHAT CAN I DO TO SEE MY FAITH STRENGTHENED?

As you read what I've written you may be saying, "I want to trust my Lord more fully. What can I do? What is my part?" Let me make several suggestions.

First, *recognize your personal obstacles to trusting our Lord.* I've mentioned individuals who grew up in skeptical, cynical environments. Be honest about how you have been conditioned to unbelief. You may have had painful experiences where someone made promises and then let you down, and you determined that you wouldn't trust anyone again. Or, you may have had others project an image of God as a senile, ineffective, distant or vengeful person. It is hard to trust that kind of person.

For some the obstacle may be an ignorance of what the Bible really teaches about our Lord. It's almost impossible to trust someone you don't know. For you a realistic plan to get to know who he is and the commitments he has made to you will be important. The more his words — especially his promises — are readily available to your mind the more you can choose to trust what he has promised.

This leads me to a second suggestion. *Read, study, memorize and meditate on who your heavenly Father is and what he has promised you.* I've mentioned the Psalms study earlier. That's a good place to begin. Another helpful thing to do is study the names of our Lord. They reveal great insights about who he is. When Jesus was in the garden of Gethsemane, prior to going to the cross he prayed for the disciples. He said "I have manifested your name to the men whom you gave me" (John 17:6), and then said, "The words which you gave me I have given to them" (17:8). He recognized the truth I'm sharing with you: knowledge of our heavenly Father is crucial to trusting him.

I came to trust Jesus Christ when I was twelve years old. For over five decades I've maintained a habit of reading the Bible over and over. In those early years I began to memorize verses that spoke to me about my Lord, who he is and what he has promised. This storehouse of biblical facts has helped me in indescribable ways to keep my focus on him and to trust him for all things. I cannot emphasize enough the importance of your life being rooted solidly in biblical truth!

My third suggestion is to *begin to take steps of trust, based on his promise.* The way this has worked for me is to find clear statements in the Bible about who he is or what he has promised.

Prayerfully I say something like this: "Father, you have said in your word that (read or quote that specific thing the Bible says). I believe that you are a person who speaks truthfully. Today I'm choosing to believe that you meant what you said and I'm going to trust you to fulfill that promise."

If I'm tempted to doubt or draw back I remind myself that my Lord is faithful and cannot deny his commitments, and that I intend to live by that commitment.

Jeremiah was an Old Testament prophet who experienced much hardship and discouragement. At one very difficult point in his life he said, "So I say, 'My strength has perished, and so has my hope from the Lord'" (Lam. 3:18). But then just a few verses later he makes a very significant statement:

> This I recall to my mind, therefore I have hope.
> The Lord's lovingkindnesses indeed never cease,
> For His compassions never fail.
> They are new every morning; great is Thy faithfulness,
> "The Lord is my portion," says my soul.
> "Therefore I have hope in Him."
> (3:21-24 NASB).

Isn't that an amazing reminder to you and me? Jeremiah got so discouraged that he felt hopeless. Then he recalled what he knew to be true about his Lord. And this renewed his faith, and strengthened him to face the difficult place he was in.

FOR REFLECTION

1. Place yourself on this continuum of faith

←——————————————————————————————→

Little faith   Strong faith

2. What past life circumstances have shaped your tendency to trust or not trust others?

3. What in this chapter has challenged you to become stronger in trusting our Lord?

4. What questions still remain in your mind concerning trusting your Lord?

8.

THE REAL IDENTITY THEFT

I listened today as two of the Lord God's children were speaking. One kept speaking of himself as a "sinner saved by grace." The person seemed to have no sense that he was now a chosen child of the King of the Kingdom. I didn't hear anything about him being a redeemed, sanctified saint. I felt a sense of sadness that this child of the King had no awareness of his royal heritage. I wondered if he would live more joyful and victorious if he knew who he really was.

I often ponder what causes these redeemed earthlings to continue to see themselves as baptized heathen rather than redeemed citizens of the Eternal Kingdom. What a difference to sit at the King's table and partake as a cherished child. Their Father is seeking royal family members, not paupers. I'm mystified why they don't see that.

— Diary of a Puzzled Angel

WHO AM I ANYWAY?

Each day when I arrive at the fitness center I am required to show the attendant my membership card and valid identification. So I pull out my driver's license, the attendant looks at my photo and then I'm allowed to go to my workout. If I couldn't identify myself I'd be turned away. This same process occurs when I go to the airport to check my luggage and get a seat assignment. If I can't prove my identity I'll be turned away. If I were to go to an ATM to take money from my bank account I'd have to have my bank identification card and my own PIN number that proves to the machine that I'm the person who owns that account. Otherwise, no money!

In our technological age we have simplified identity to assigning a person their own number as a convenient way of establishing identity. My first identity number was my social security card. When I joined the Navy I was assigned a military ID number. In college the administration knew me by my student ID number. Now I have a credit card number, health care patient number, driver's license number, and more. Each number represents a different piece of "who I am" and remembering which number goes with which identity can get confusing.

As big a nuisance as these various impersonal ID's are, what is even scarier is the thought of someone snatching my wallet, or getting my social security number and "stealing" my identity. From what I've heard from others who have had this happen it is a nightmare. The phone rings and the voice on the other end says, "Are you Norm Wakefield?" I say, "Yes," and then I'm informed that I have a charge for a new automobile that I've purchased. I'm shocked because I haven't bought a new car. But someone else using my identity did and now I have the annoying task of proving that it wasn't me, but an impostor.

So identity is a big deal.

Now imagine that you are seated around a table with a group of six strangers. One person says, "We're going to be together for the next several days so let's go around the table and identify ourselves." When you're turn came would you say, "I'm delighted to be here. I'm 323 43 6180," reciting your social security number. If you did that everyone would laugh and think inwardly, "She's a nut." What you're more likely to do is to give your name, where you live and some fact about where you work, whether you're married or not, etc. By that act you've said that your identity is your name and place of dwelling. But is that all there is to you? Is that the most important way to identify the essence of who you are?

But then Sue, one of the group members, gives everyone a piece of paper. On the sheet are the words, "I am . . ." listed ten times with space between each entry to complete the statement. "I'd like you to complete the ten 'I am's'" Sue says, "Each time saying something different about yourself. Put the first thoughts that come to your mind that describe who you are." As you try to complete the task you find it hard to say ten things about yourself. What appears as a simple assignment is actually quite hard. "What do I say that tells these strangers who I really am — the real me?"

HOW DO I DETERMINE WHO I REALLY AM?

To fully enjoy the amazing Father-child relationship we've received we have to get correct answers to three important questions. The first is *"Who is this person we call Father?"* What is the essence of this individual we call the Lord, God, the Almighty or Father? Is he strong or weak, intelligent or ignorant, personal or impersonal, loving or vindictive, etc. Then we face a second question, *"Who do I perceive my heavenly Father to be in relationship to me."* These first two questions cause us to discover what the Bible says about our Lord and how he has indicated that he intends to relate to us. But even if we can answer those questions accurately we still have to face a third puzzler before we can live in totally harmony with our beloved Father.

For the third question I have to ask, *"Who do I perceive myself to be?"* (Not "Who am I?" but "Who do I perceive myself to be?" That may sound like a strange question. One reason it is strange is because most of us haven't asked ourselves that question. In a sense it is embarrassing because we have to talk about ourselves and many of us are uncomfortable doing that. A second reason is that we've had so much input from others that we are either confused or threatened by what we think we'll find. Nevertheless the answer to this third question is as important as the first two for shaping the way we live out our existence on this planet.

Actually, there is another question behind the third one we've asked. When I ask myself, "Who am I? I have to ask, "How did I determine who I am?" That's why I emphasized the word perceive. We tend to think that we came to a decision about who we are by some objective method. But the truth is that we can't answer it in isolation because we can only discover who we are in relationship with other people. Otherwise we have no means to measure ourselves. If I say,"I'm the stupidest person alive," I'll be measuring myself by others I know who appear to me to be more intelligent.

Let's create a scenario to see this more clearly. Imagine that you were on a trip and were involved in an automobile accident. You are now in a hospital and have been in a coma for two weeks. As you come out of the coma you have no memory of who you are. You can't even remember your name. The attending nurse says, "You were in an automobile accident, but didn't have any identification on you. Who are you?"

How would you answer?

All you could say would be, "I don't know who I am." You don't know
- your name
- your age
- your family background
- where you live
- how intelligent you are
- what your athletic ability is
- your occupation
- your socio-economic status
- your strengths or weaknesses

But a day after you've emerged from the coma a stranger stands beside your bed. "I'm your father," he says with tears streaming down his cheeks. "You can't imagine how I've suffered not knowing whether you were alive or dead. I've come to care for you and take you home." Then he sits down in a chair by your bedside and tells you *who you are*. What he tells you about yourself becomes the basis for your identity. In a very real sense you become who he tells you, if you believe that he is telling you the truth.

The ironic thing is that he could be an impostor, telling you lies about yourself, and he'd still be forming your identity if you believed him, and you probably would.

Now we've arrived at an important insight. What we've come to believe about ourselves has been largely formed by what others have assigned to us. And what they have told us can as easily be false as it is true.

GETTING A SECOND CHANCE AT LIFE

A few years ago I was studying the life of the apostle Paul and discovered something that changed my life. As I read the third chapter of Philippians I heard the apostle describing who he saw himself to be prior to his encounter with Jesus Christ. Paul tells us that he was very proud of his heritage and accomplishments. In fact he lists them for his readers to review. Here were his credentials (I've added my commentary in italics):

> • circumcised on the eighth day. *I was born into a godly home and dedicated to the Jewish faith at birth.*
> • of the people of Israel. *I am of a nation chosen of God. We considered ourselves his special, privileged people.*
> • of the tribe of Benjamin. *Benjaminites were fierce warriors. I have a heritage of courage. Nobody pushes us around.*
> • a Hebrew of Hebrews. *I modeled the Hebrew traditions and was a blue-blood Hebrew.*
> • in regards of the law, a Pharisee. *I achieved the highest position of honor and respect in the Jewish community. People looked up to me. I was the epitome of religious godliness. Young men wanted to be like me when they grew up.*
> • as for zeal, persecuting the church. *I was no slacker. I put my faith into practice, rooting out those who opposed our Jewish beliefs with fierce determination. I lived my convictions.*

- as for legalistic righteousness, faultless. *I was the model of religious dedication. I lived a faultless life.*

As I thought about Paul's words it struck me that all of these marks that told him who he was were what his society identified as marks of significance. Nowhere has our Lord ever said that these were his ways of seeing us. We have no reason to believe that they were of any importance to Him. In fact, some of society's positive marks might be negatives to our Lord. Paul's marks were cultural marks and they had shaped who this Pharisee determined he was. As he walked down the streets of his hometown he'd feel proud and important. He might have said to himself, "I'm an important person--somebody significant in the nation. People admire me, look up to me and listen to me." Prior to his conversion Paul had determined who he was by his culture, not by what our Lord had said. He viewed himself by what he had achieved, the position he held, and his religious heritage.

And you and I do the same thing!

But let's get back to Paul. He next graphically describes a radical conversion that took place in his mind. Paul had a paradigm shift. Prior to his conversion he saw himself in a certain way; after his conversion he saw himself in a totally different way. He tells us "But whatever gain I had, I counted as loss for the sake of Christ. Indeed, I count everything as loss because of the surpassing worth of knowing Christ Jesus my Lord. For his sake I have suffered the loss of all things and count them as rubbish, in order that I may gain Christ and be found in him, not having a righteousness of my own that comes from the law, but that which comes through faith in Christ, the righteousness from God that depends on faith" (Phil. 3:7-9). Do you grasp the magnitude of what he is saying? He tells us that those marks that identified him prior to encountering Jesus Christ now have no significance to him. He swept them up, dumped them in the garbage pail, and replaced them with a totally new way of answering the "Who am I?" question. (It's interesting that he even changed his name.) From that day forward Paul allowed only one Person to be the authority on that question—his Lord.

Now with the slate wiped clean Paul replaces it with a totally new perspective; he sees himself in a radically different light. If you ask him "Who are you," he will never give you the old answers. They've been erased and replaced with a new inner reality about himself that powerfully transformed his perception and behavior. He is a transformed man because Paul chooses to see himself as his Lord sees him.

This is why the Apostle Paul could say to the Corinthian believers, "Therefore, if anyone is in Christ, he is a new creation; the old has gone, the new has come!" (II Cor. 5:17).

Can you say—with conviction—what Paul says?

WHO DOES MY LORD SAY I AM?

The verse I've cited above gives us the first clue as to how our heavenly Father identifies us. He sees us in Christ. Robert McQuilkin helps us see the importance of this new reality:

> The two concepts of His indwelling us and our living in Him both focus on a relationship of identity of life, of belonging.
>
> To be "in Christ" is to be possessed by Him, and to possess Him, in an intimate, loving identity of mutual commitment. It is like the Hebrew concept of knowing. As a man knew his wife, so with

being "in Christ." The initial bonding is for two
lovers in an intimate relationship.[1]

Our Lord says that we have a new relationship and he
always sees us in this new relationship. He always sees us "in
Christ" and that is the beginning point for us to view ourselves.
We are no longer the sum of all that other people on this earth
have said we were, but in a remarkable way we really are intimately connected to Jesus Christ. Our heavenly Father always
sees us intimately joined to Christ and that's how he tells us to
see ourselves.

Oswald Chambers says, "When I am born again, the Spirit
of God takes me right out of myself and my experiences, and
identifies me with Jesus Christ. If I am left with my experiences,
my expereinces have not been produced by Redemption."[2]

This new reality leads me beyond myself, freeing me from
evaluating myself by my heritage, achievements, socio-economic
standing, and more.If you want to be convinced of this truth
find a Bible concordance and look up the phrases, "in Christ,"
"by Christ" and "through Christ." I guarantee that you will find
an abundance of statements that describe our lives as connected
to him in this delightful, devoted way. Jesus himself talked
about this in John 15 when he says that we are to live in him just
as a branch is intimately and securely connected to the vine. He
then assures us that our lives will bear abundant fruit as a natural outcome of this union.

When Paul uses this language he makes statements like:

- we are joint-heirs with Christ (Rom. 8:17)
- we are grounded and established in Christ (2
Cor. 1:21)
- we are caused to triumph in Christ (2 Cor. 2:14)

- we have been baptized into Christ (Col. 3:27)
- we have all spiritual blessing in Christ (Eph. 1:3)
- we share in his promises in Christ (Eph. 3:6)

It's obvious that this is not some theological jargon that Paul dreams up to prove that he is some brainy guy. Rather it is a powerful truth about the new person we've become by this God-ordained bonding to his beloved Son. So the most accurate way to respond to "Who are you?" is to say, "I am a person insepara-bly bonded to Jesus Christ and my eternal Father says that I am 'in him.' The old ways that marked my life are now invalid to him and so they are not valid identification marks to me either.

The implications of this truth are mind-boggling. Everything that I loved or hated about myself — and others — is tossed into the rubbish heap. Who I am and how I choose to see others is profoundly redefined. When Paul commented on this to the Galatian Christians he reminded them that their true identity was as God's children, individuals who had been "clothed" with Christ (Gal. 3:27). Because of this he said that the old way of de-fining ourselves is obsolete. No more Jew or Greek — away with ethnic or national distinctions. No more slave or free — away with hierarchical distinctions. No more male or female — away with gender distinctions. (v. 28) In society these bases for com-parison will remain. But for the child of God they are removed to allow new bases for relationships. We are united as brothers and sisters in our Father's family. That supersedes the other identifying marks.

TRANSFORMING TRUTH VS. ESOTERIC TRUTH

A number of years ago my friends, Jill and Matthew Bachali,

went to Viet Nam to adopt a son they named Henry. While conversing with the birth mother they were astonished to discover that Henry had a twin brother. Upon returning to the United States with Henry they began the procedure to adopt the brother. After a few months Matthew flew back to Viet Nam believing he could complete the adoption process. To his and Jill's grief the mother wanted money to purchase the second child. Since such a practice was illegal, with great sorrow my friend returned home empty-handed.

Young Henry now has a new set of parents, a new home, a new name, a new brother and sister, a new language, and a new nationality. He may look Vietnamese, but his whole life has already been transformed with a new identity because a man and woman "redeemed" him from a former life to a new life. The old life is gone and he will grow up in the new. But the "unredeemed" twin brother won't have a new identity like Henry.

Those who have been redeemed by Jesus Christ have as new an identity as the Bachali's son. The Word of God makes this clear. The apostle Paul demonstrated by every fiber of his being that a revolutionary transformation had occurred in the way his Lord viewed him, how he viewed himself and how he expected others to view him. This transformation wasn't something to sit around the campfire and debate intellectually. It was a truth that gripped his life and changed everything about how he lived. That's the defining evidence that the truth had set him free.

Is this the way this remarkable truth impacts your life and mine? Do we live as new persons who have moved from an old lifestyle rooted in an old way of seeing ourselves that was defined by our world? Or, are we still living by the marks of success or failure that we learned from our earthly existence? The answer to those two questions indicates how much we believe that we are new persons bonded to Jesus Christ.

FOR REFLECTION

1. Write down four statements that describe who you are. Begin each one with "I am..."?

2. Which of the above are "old" identity statements or "new" statements about who you are as God's child? Why is this an important issue?

3. List five statements that identify who our Lord has said you are. What would it take for you to live those truths?

4. How would the Lord introduce you to an angel? What would He say about who you are?

9.

LOVE'S MANY DEFINITIONS

Wow! How mixed up these earthlings are about love! They talk about loving everything from French fries, to new cars, to the Lord. But what's sad is their distorted view about their heavenly Father and his unconditional love for them. It must make him grieve to see how his children twist his love and make it so small and puny. If they could only see how high, how wide, how deep and how long his love is it would — to use one of their phrase — blow their minds.

I'm also puzzled at why those who claim to know the Bible so well keep putting doubts in their follower's minds about how much the Sovereign One loves them. They teach and preach a conditional love.

Don't they know that He loves them because of who he is, not because of what they do. I'm baffled.

— Diary of a Puzzled Angel

YOUR BEGINNING TASKS

In order to gain the most from this chapter I'd like you to do two things before you read further. First, pause from your reading and write out your definition of love. Do that now, right here:

"I define love as . . .

Now that you've finished the first task do a second thing: Think about a time when you experienced being loved by someone (other than our Lord).

For example, I remember the first time anyone threw a surprise birthday party for me. I was in my early twenties and I assumed that I was going to a young adult event at church. A friend asked me to help him carry some chairs from another room for the meeting. When I went into the room and turned on the overhead light I was startled to hear my friends holler, "Surprise!" It scared the wits out of me, but I felt warm inside to know that someone thought I was special and planned this event to demonstrate it. And by the way, the person who planned that loving event later became my wife!

Now it's your turn. Stop reading and write down that experience in the space provided here:

MY CHILD, I LOVE YOU

The most important love affair we'll ever experience is between our heavenly Father and us as his children. Unfortunately, many of us can recite Bible verses that tell how much he loves us (Such as, "God demonstrates his own love for us in this: While we were still sinners, Christ died for us." Rom. 5:8) but can't resurrect examples of times when it became a tangible reality. Long after I'd memorized verses like the one I've just mentioned, I lived with a haunting sense that I was a nuisance to my Lord, giving him migraine headaches. I lived as though God didn't love me. He didn't even *like me*. I had a *dictionary* definition, but not an *experiential* definition

But he kept pursuing me, forcing me to recognize that his love was spectacular, persistent and genuine,

I recall one such incident where I was confronted with his love. It occurred in the early years of my marriage.

My wife Winnie and I, along with our first three preschool-aged children, were moving from Portsmouth, Virginia to Wheaton, Illinois. All our earthly belongings were crammed in a U-Haul trailer that was hitched behind our 64 Falcon automobile. About fifty miles into our 800 mile journey I faced the sinking feeling that the trailer was too heavy for the automobile to tow and we had 750 more miles to go. I couldn't turn back and I didn't know how I would get my family and our possessions to that distant destination.

I felt frightened, discouraged, drained and helpless.

Two days later I was sitting in church with my family, feeling the impact of the previous days' trauma. A loving father-in-law had helped me find a way to continue on our journey. Now seated in that church pew it seemed that every hymn had been personally selected by my heavenly Father to affirm his faithful love for me. His touching care for me and my family was undeniable. I couldn't restrain the tears if I wanted to. I knew that this tender, compassionate Father knew my need and reached out to lovingly affirm that my family and I were fondly and safely held in his tender arms.

Unfortunately many of us live by our dictionary definitions of love (which I asked you to write out at the beginning of this chapter). It may be technically accurate but practically meaningless. Our daily experience reveals that we don't have an experiential definition that leaves us with joy, peace and an inner sense of being treasured by this loving Father. We may have been grounded in teaching that portrayed him as a stern taskmaster that was squeezing every bit of labor and pure behavior out of us as payment for our salvation. Or, we may have grown up in such a barren, love starved environment that we wouldn't recognize love if it walked right passed us. Or, we may have lived lives saturated with failure, sin and foolishness that leads us to feel disqualified to be loved.

I've been reminding you throughout this book that what you understand as the terms or conditions of your relationship with your beloved Father will shape that relationship. It's inevitable that we've formed our paradigm of love from the composite of our life experience and teaching. What others have modeled and said, and what life circumstances I've encountered are then projected onto this eternal relationship. So we incorporate a concept of our Lord loving us into our earthly paradigm of love.

That's an unfortunate error because it will leave us short of knowing the beauty, wonder, power and awe of his Father love. As I've said earlier, our challenge is to let him teach us what his paradigm looks like. What is his reality? And his reality will be radically different from what we've learned in this world. This Father love is so radically different from anything we've experienced here on earth that the apostle Paul says we'll never be able to fathom its heights, depths, breadth, or length (Eph. 3:19).

Our danger is that we are so inundated with the word "love" that we think we know what it means when related to our Lord. But sadly our culture dilutes its richness so we can associate love with pencils, television programs, sports heroes, toothpaste, etc.

We have to shift into his paradigm of reality and let God teach us the wonder of his Father heart—unlike anything we've ever known—if we are going to begin plumbing its bottom-less depths. But every new understanding and experience of it transforms us more and more into more joyous, satisfied, restful individuals.

FATHERLOVE: WHAT IS IT?

Whatever you think you know about our heavenly Father's love for you, it is deficient!

How could I make such a seemingly rude, offensive state-ment? I do it without fear of error because his love is so vast, so profound, so unique that no person on earth can assimilate its wonder, richness and depth.

Chip Ingram expresses it well:

> I'm convinced that God's love is one of the hard-
> est attributes for us to get a handle on. I've seen
> glimpses of it, but like most of us, my under-
> standing falls short. I've done my biblical home-
> work, and I know what the passages say, but I
> find myself even more tongue-tied than when I
> try to explain to my wife what I mean when I say

"I love you." I never sense that I've done a very good job explaining it. In the same way, explaining God's love always turns into describing what is far better, deeper, and wider than words can capture. [1]

Remember, our Lord's love flows from a totally different paradigm of reality than ours. Discovering the love that comes from his paradigm is a lifelong adventure. The more we ponder what the Bible reveals about it the more we realize that we'll never absorb its fullness until we see him face to face. (And perhaps we won't be able to grasp it's enormity even then.)

As a means to stress how different his love is I'm going to coin this new word:

Fatherlove.

When you read this word remind yourself that this is his unique love, higher, deeper, wider and longer than any we've experienced on this earth. *It's not just a "souped up" version of human love; it comes from a different source which means that we must look at it as something new.*

Thankfully the Word of God gives a wealth of insight about the nature of our Father's love for us. From cover to cover he is repeatedly shouting out his love in words and actions that defy comprehension. We can water it down by filtering it through our past teaching and understanding but that is what I'm challenging you not to do. Thus, the more we read about it, meditate on it and allow it to penetrate our hearts and minds the more we will respond to his loving actions toward us. We'll learn to bask in it and let it penetrate to the depths of our soul.

In the following pages I identify what I'll call "love principles" that highlight some of the essence of Fatherlove. They should form the bases for our relationship with our loving Lord.

They show you how utterly different his love is from what we have known and experienced.

Occasionally we'll meet someone whose love for others shines brightly, but when compared with our heavenly Father's love it is very dim. It's like comparing the light of the sun and the moon.

LOVE PRINCIPLE 1: FATHERLOVE IS UNIQUE

Fatherlove is unique because it is rooted in who he is not because of who we are.

When I state this principle I'm reminded of a *Dennis the Menace* cartoon in which Dennis and his buddy are walking down the sidewalk with a cookie in their hands. He says to his friend, "Mrs. Wilson gives you a cookie because she's nice, not because you're nice."

When the apostle John addresses the subject of our Lord's love he says, "Whoever does not love does not know God, because God is love (I John 4:8).

Notice that John does not say "God loves," but rather "God is love." He affirms this thought a few verses later when he tells his readers, "God is love, Whoever lives in love lives in God, and God in him (v. 16).

Do you recognize the vast difference in the nature of our Father's love and human love?

We love because we've been taught to love. It's a behavior we've learned or an attitude we've cultivated. And if we are truthful we are more apt to love individuals who are warm, friendly and agreeable. We have to work at loving the ornery, cantankerous person, or that person who gives nothing in return. But no one had to teach God to love because *it's an aspect of his nature – integral to who he is*. As the Bible speaks of how his love expresses itself we discover an unlimited abundance of supply.

Our Lord can never run out of love because his love is who he is. In Romans 5:5 it is likened to a never diminishing fountain that gushes forth with deliciously refreshing water. We are told that "God has poured out his love into our hearts by the Holy Spirit, whom he has given us."

Whenever I think of this I think of a spring near my grand-parent's farmhouse. It came out of the hillside and ran into a milkhouse. From there it ran on to a watering trough. The spring never ceased running. Any person who wanted a drink of cool, refreshing water could drink freely from this source. Whether a dedicated preacher or an evil bank robber the spring offered its refreshment to all. The spring issued this pure sustenance because that was its nature, not because someone deserved it.

Consider these aspects of this fathomless love:

Fatherlove is wholistic.

He loves us in his thoughts. He loves us with an emotion. He loves us in his actions. Any way our Father relates to us will be soaked with his love. Even when he disciplines us it is with this same depth of devotion.

Fatherlove is passionate.

In a most remarkable passage in the book of Hosea our Father describes his feelings toward his wandering children — the Israelites. Listen to his own love-saturated lament.

> When Israel was a child, I love him, and out of
> Egypt I called by son. But the more I called Israel,
> the further they went from me, They sacrificed to
> the Baals and they burned incense to images. It
> was I who taught Ephraim to walk, taking them
> by the arms; but they did not reality it was I who

healed them. I led them with cords of human
kindness with ties of love; I lifted the yoke from
their neck and bent down to feed them.
(Hosea 11:1-4)

Can you feel the burning intensity of our Lord's passion and
devotion to people who have thumbed their nose at him and
insult him by worshipping idols? How would we respond if our
children treated us this way? Now listen again to his amazing
confession of love.

"How can I give up, Ephraim? How can I
hand you over, Israel? How can I treat you like
Admah? How can I make you like Zeboiim? My
heart is changed within me; all my compassion is
aroused. I will not carry out my fierce anger, nor
will I turn and devastate Ephraim. For I am God,
and not man" (vv. 8, 9).

Can you hear our Lord's passionate love for his wayward
people? Can you hear his Father heart beating fervently and af-
fectionately from the depths of his loving heart? Let's move on.

Fatherlove is tender. One of the touching description the
Psalmist uses to describe our Lord's love is the word translated
in the NASB "lovingkindness."

"Remember, O Lord, Thy compassion and Thy lovingkind-
nesses, for they have been from of old" (Psa. 25:6 NASB).

"Thy lovingkindness and Thy truth will continually preserve
me" (Psa. 40:11 NASB).

"Who crowns you with lovingkindness and compassion"
(Psa. 103:4 NASB).

This Fatherlove is unique in that it doesn't seek someone worthy of his love, but his love gives great significance to our lives. We must begin to understand the greatness of that truth each day or the experience that truth, personally, in God's presence, may be difficult for us to obtain.

LOVE PRINCIPLE 2: FATHERLOVE IS A GIFT

I took a break from writing this chapter to spend an hour or so with a seminary student. He came to my house toting his three-month-old daughter in a baby carrier. After forty-five minutes had passed she became agitated and began to cry. When my friend lovingly picked her up and cuddled her to his chest she quieted down and began to coo and smile. Then we began to talk about how his father love would impact her life as she grew through childhood and into adulthood. How secure she would feel. How valued. How cherished.

I have friends who have adopted children. It cost them a bundle financially. It required adjustments to their lifestyle. But I never heard one of them say, "What'll I get out of this? What's my payoff?" Rather they exhibited behaviors that made me think that they were the luckiest people on the face of the earth to receive this special gift. And children who grow up with such love know that they are cherished and valued in the eyes of their parents.

What makes our Lord's love so profound and different is that it is lavished on those who are unlovely, those who have nothing to contribute to him, those who have lived degrading lives and wasted what was entrusted to them. The truth is that none of us have anything that would profit our Lord. The astounding fact is that he loved us when we were at our worst. One of the snares that hindered my relationship with our Father was the belief that I needed to earn his love. And I never could do that because I was always failing the test. I can never thank him enough for loving me at my worst as generously as for loving me when I'm at my best.

For years I've returned to Romans 5 to ponder this utterly different kind of love. The writer, the apostle Paul, goes to great pains to assure us of our hopeless condition. First, he states that "when we were still powerless, Christ died for the godly" (v. 6). This love was lavished on us when we have no strength — we could do *nothing* for him. We were powerless to contribute anything. Second, Paul ups the ante by saying two verses later that "God demonstrated his own love for us in this: While we were still sinners, Christ died for us" (v. 8). So now we are not only weak, helpless, powerless, but we also are sinners. We're missing the mark. We're violating his rules. We are those who have violated every good thing our Lord stands for. Yet his love is showered on us *while we were sinners.*

But Paul is not done. He adds a third reason why this love is so incredible. In Romans 5:10 he tells us that "when we were God's *enemies,* we were reconciled to him through the death of his Son" (italics added). Fatherlove is available to those who are helpless failures, to those who are sinners, and even to those who opposed him and were identified as his enemies. It's obvious that this love finds nothing deserving in us. It's also obvious that this love is wholly different than the best human love can muster up.

Fatherlove is a devoted, passionate love given to us as a pure gift. He gives it with no strings attached. After over sixty years of walking with him I still find this breathtaking. In fact, the longer I live the more I marvel at such an indescribable love.

Someone related a story to me several years ago that I have never forgotten. A Christian man was very ill. During the time when he was trying to recover he had opportunity to reflect on the way he had lived his life. When one of his friends came to visit him he shared this reflection and lamented how little love he discovered in his heart for his Lord.

After hearing him out his friend spoke.

"When I leave here I will go home to be with my family. When I enter my home I'll look for my little baby and eagerly take her in my arms. Then I'll look into her precious face, be thrilled by her smile and listen to her chatter. As tired as I am her presence will give me great joy and my heart will be warmed."

He continued. "The truth is her love for me is probably non-existent. If I were overwhelmed with sorrow it wouldn't bother her one bit. If I were suffering agonizing bodily pain she'd go right on playing with her playthings. If I died she'd forget me in a matter of days and go on with life. The truth is this little child is a great expense to me and will continue to be so for years to come."

"My friend, I don't have much money in the bank, but no amount of money could purchase this little one from me. Though she is a great expense I'd never give her up. Why? Does she love me, or do I love her? Do you think I'd withhold my love until I know that she's capable of loving me? Would I wait for her to do something that would merit my love before I'd grant her mine?"

Because I am the father of five adult children and eight grandchildren I can identify fully with what this man told his ailing friend. I have a close friend who has reared his children through great personal emotional, physical and financial cost. (I've been especially aware of his emotional pain). Yet many times I've heard him say with deep emotion, "I love each one of them. Each is precious to me." The apostle John penned the following words, "This is real love. It is not that we loved God, but that he loved us and sent his Son as a sacrifice to take away our sins" (I John 4;10 NLT).

LOVE PRINCIPLE 3: FATHERLOVE LIBERATES & TRANSFORMS

Fatherlove is unique because by its very nature its liberates us from shame, guilt and condemnation and transforms us into lovers.

One of the great passages that speaks of our Lord's love is found in Eph. 5:25. The context is Paul's admonition to husbands to love their wives. In doing so he draws from this profound Fatherlove that was revealed through Christ. Paul urges husbands to love their wives, "just as Christ loved the church and gave himself up for her to make her holy, cleansing her by the washing with water through the word and to present her to himself as a radiant church, without stain or wrinkle or any other blemish, but holy and blameless."

He's speaking of a love that is so powerful, so penetrating, so overwhelming that it will transform us. Those who drink deeply of this free gift of love can never remain the same. It's obvious that most of us know little of this life changing love. When we plunge into our Father's abundant, compassionate, tender, caring love and drink lavishly from its fountain it is impossible to ever again be satisfied with whatever the world has to offer. Everything looks, taste and feels bland and unfulfilling.

Occasionally I'll meet a person who becomes agitated when he hears me speak of this unconditional, free, passionate love of our heavenly Father. The person is fearful that people will take advantage of it. The person worries that our Lord will be exploited. But I assure you just as I assure that person, when we drink deeply of Fatherlove it will not prompt us to sin; it will draw us to holiness. The real problem is we don't understand the nature of our Father's love so we keep attaching conditions or terms to it and it disgraces our Lord. We make him small and manipulative like ourselves.

The apostle Paul understood this truth very well. When he prayed for the Ephesian Christians he asked that they would be *rooted* and *established* in this profound love. He asked that they would *grasp* its width, length, height and depth. He prayed that they would *know the unknowable*. He caps his request off by asking these followers would be *filled to the measure of all the fullness of God* (Eph, 3:14-20). Now I ask you, could a person experience this incredible relationship of love as Paul describes it and remain the same? Would not this intense, intimate Fatherlove change the person forever?

Fatherlove a gift he wants you to experience: Given generously, freely, without strings attached. Like the spring at Grandpa Learn's farm all I have to do is come and drink freely. But remember, knowing about my grandfather's spring is not the same as drinking from it. In the same way knowing about your Father's love is not the same as receiving that love and letting it touch the deepest parts of your being. But I warn you, if you *really* drink freely you'll find yourself returning more and more frequently because you'll never find anything that satisfies, renews and changes you like Fatherlove. And one day you'll realize that you've become a container of this heavenly nectar that spills over into other people's lives.

Your Father's love is . . .

- intentional
- unconditional
- irrevocable
- irresistible
- undefeatable.

FOR REFLECTION

O my God, possess my soul with such an ardent
love of Thee, so buoyant above all other affections, that no one may ever come in competition
with it; such a love as may not only subdue all
other affections, but purify and make them innocent; such a love as may create in my soul a
perpetual pleasure in the contemplation of Thee,
and a continual thirst after Thee; a love which
may transport my soul with Thy divine perfec-
tions, and paint there such bright ideas of Thy
glorious majesty, that none of the trifling pleasures and temptations of this world may be able
to make on it the least impression.[2]

— Hom. Charles Howe , Esq. (1661-1745)

+++

1. What life experiences have shaped your view of love?

2. What in this chapter challenges your view of God's love for you?

3. Compare and contrast Fatherlove with human love.

4. What examples can you think of from Christ's life on earth that demonstrate his loving heart?

5. Imagine that Jesus were sitting beside you on a sofa. What would you be feeling? Explain.

10.

SNAPSHOTS OF DAD

Sometimes I wish I could go to earth and tell those followers of the Sovereign One who he really is. I know that he sent his Son to reveal who he is, but since then no one seems to realize what an amazing person he is. It seems as though they want to make him a carbon copy of their earthly fathers. They sing songs about his greatness and recite verses from the Holy Book, but continue to act as though he was like them.

I wish they could see his surpassing greatness, his limitless love, his incomparable faithfulness, his spectacular beauty. How it grieves me to see his followers continue to limit the Holy One. How heavy my heart is when I see them live such shallow lives when he offers them so much. If only they knew. I'm perplexed.

— Diary of a Puzzled Angel

HOW I DISCOVERED MY REAL FATHER

The apostle Paul must have been a mighty man of prayer. His prayers have insight, depth and passion. When he prayed for the Ephesian Christians he said that he knelt "before the Father, from whom his whole family in heaven and on earth derives its name" (Eph. 3:14). Paul sees that our Father in heaven is the original — the prototype — from which earthly fathers find their model. Unfortunately we reverse the order letting our relationship with our earthly father define our heavenly Father. Unscrambling and clarifying the difference is an essential part of coming to know the truth of this joyful, eternal relationship.

I stumbled on a way to distinguish the two fathers quite by accident. One day I decided to work through the Psalms noting every reference to the Lord — my Father. So whenever I noted a verse or verses that spoke of him in some way I marked a "L" in front of it to indicate that it told me something about my ultimate Father. I slowly worked my way through the 150 Psalms marking each appropriate entry until I have covered all of them.

Next, I opened my notebook and wrote at the top of a clean sheet of paper "My heavenly Father is . . ." Returning to the Psalms I began to scan from the beginning watching for my coded "L's." After I read the entry I'd write in my notebook a statement about what that verse told me about my Father. For example, Psalm 9:9 says, "The LORD is a stronghold for the oppressed, a stronghold in times of trouble." For that entry I wrote "My heavenly Father is a place of safety and security for me in times of trouble. He is delighted when I turn to him for help."

But I also wanted to check up on myself to see if this truth was a personal reality, or merely a piece of factual information to be stored in my mental computer. So I closed my eyes after that entry and asked myself, "Is this real to me? Do I run to

Father when trouble occurs and find this a place of emotional safety?" If I could say "yes" I'd place a "Y" in front of the entry. If my response was "No" I'd place a "N" before it. In that way I became aware of:

• new truths about my Father I was discovering,
• old truths about him that were real in my life,
• old truths that I'd learned, but which were not working in my life.

The exercise I've just described proved to be far more significant than I thought it would be. In many ways it gave me a tangible way to view my relationship with my heavenly Father. It sensitized me to truths that I'd wholeheartedly embrace, but which were not meaningful in my daily experience. I now had a better handle on aspects of the relationship that needed to be developed. I could see where the relationship was alive, vital and fulfilling, and where it was unsatisfying or inoperative.

But I gained another valuable gift from this exercise. A "profile" of my heavenly father began to emerge. I realized that until this time I didn't have a mental "snapshot" of who he was. Up until then I only had a hodge podge of scattered data. It was more like doing a study of George Washington and knowing information about him. But the Psalms exercise moved me more into knowing him, not just knowing about him. I discovered in the Psalms a wonderful profile of my heavenly Father that highlights his beauty, character, power and devoted care for each child in his family.

WHAT I LEARNED ABOUT MY REAL FATHER

This delightful investigation of the Psalms made me aware of significant themes about our Father that reoccurred throughout the book. I found that I could group them in ways that helped me focus my mental camera and take a snapshot of Father in action. I'd like to highlight some of the dominant qualities of his profile the Psalms gives us:

Father is the one who provides security and safety in the midst of life's stormy trials.

All of us need a safe harbor in which to anchor our boat when life's sea is storm tossed. Even the mighty warrior, David, recognized that he needed a place of safety when life became too intense, too threatening. He was able to affirm that

> God is our refuge and strength, a very present help in trouble. Therefore we will not fear though the earth gives way, though the mountains be moved into the heart of the sea, though its waters roar and foam, though the mountains tremble at its swelling. Selah There is a river whose streams make glad the city of God, the holy habitation of the Most High.
> (Psa. 46:1-4).

The word refuge is used more that fifteen times in Psalms; strength is used over thirty times; words like helper, strong tower and hiding place occur again and again referring to our Father's protective care. Even the great "Shepherd Psalm" begins with "The Lord is my shepherd. I shall not be in want" (23:1). In Psalm 3:3 David prays, " But you, O LORD, are a shield about me,." In 27:1 he reminds us that "The LORD is the stronghold of my life; of whom shall I be afraid?"

Whenever I think of our Lord's commitment to care for us I remember an incident that involved my daughter, Jody, a number of years ago. She had just received her driver's license and was eager to drive. She asked if she could drive the family car to school. I gave her permission. About twenty minutes later I was standing by the kitchen sink looking out the window. I saw Jody drive in the carport. The front end of the car was bashed in (She had rear-ended a truck). In the brief moments before my sobbing daughter came in the house I realized what she needed the most. When we met I put my arms around her and said, "Are you okay? That's all that matters. The car can be repaired." I can truthfully say that I wanted my arms to be a refuge for Jody. And in a small way this reminds me of a much greater Father who is eager for us to rush into his arms to find protection, comfort and rest.

Father is a wise and loving counselor.

We live in a world overwhelmed with problems, conflicts and wars. We experience uncertainty in our personal lives, our marriages, our jobs, our church life, and in society in general. Who of us has not felt the need for someone who was eager and willing to listen to our questions, our indecision, and our struggles with a patient and loving ear? Who will help me sort out the issues in my life and guide me in wise decision making? Who can I turn to and know that person will be there when I need him?

David tells us. He expressed his appreciation for his Lord when he prayed, "O LORD, in the morning you hear my voice; in the morning I prepare a sacrifice for you and watch." (5:3). He has discovered that our Lord's ears are always open when we come to him for guidance and direction. He is never too busy, too tired, too preoccupied to give undivided attention to our voice. In a later Psalm David expressed how powerfully this truth motivated his own life. In 116:1, 2 he tells us, "I love the LORD, because he has heard my voice and my pleas for mercy.

Because he inclined his ear to me, therefore I will call on him as long as I live." (The word picture here is that of one who is bending over with his hand cupped to his ear to catch every word being spoken). The fact that his Lord was constantly available, constantly attuned to his cry prompted a response of love in David. He is motivated to walk with him during his days on earth "because he turned his ear to me."

Our Father clearly expresses his commitment to be available and guide us. His word to us is "I will instruct you and teach you in the way you should go; I will counsel you with my eye upon you." (32:8). This is not the counsel of someone who is bossy and insensitive, but that of a loving Father who cares deeply about our well-being and who wants to guide us in decision making that will be wise and fruitful.

Many of us lacked this kind of father and we project onto our eternal Father this same resentment, indifference or attitude of busyness when we want someone to talk to. Studies over the past twenty years have consistently indicated that fathers spend only minutes per week with their children. In my own experience with seminary students I find significant numbers who are over-committed and find that time spent with their children is minimal. Because our earthly father was not involved in our lives we think that our heavenly Father is the same. The Psalmist reminds us that such thinking is not biblically accurate. He is a present help in our times of need.

Father is a joyous person who delights to have us near.

Was your earthly father a delight to be with? Would you rather spend time with him than with anyone else you can think of? My wife would respond with an enthusiastic "Yes!" because her dad not only loved Jesus Christ, but he loved people and found much joy in life. But I can hear many of you saying,

"Goodness sake! No! My dad is the last person I'd associate with the word 'joy.'" I've heard so many adults speak of their father in terms like, "He was never around." "We couldn't even talk at the table." "He was only interested in adult things." "He told us to straighten up and not be so silly."

If that's been your experience you might be surprised to know that our eternal Father is a joyous Father. Whenever I read what David said about him I am still filled with awe and delight. He said, "In your presence there is fullness of joy; at your right hand are pleasures forevermore." (16:11). Wow! A Father who smiles! One who laughs. One who radiates joy. A Father who likes birthday parties and celebrations.

I confess that I didn't discover that our Father was a joyous person until I was far into my adult years. The Christians I hung around with created the impression that he could never be pleased. My own paradigm of God was that of a stern, no nonsense person who was all business. But one day I began to notice that the word joy was in the Bible. And the more I looked the more I became aware that the word was used over and over again to speak of a joyous, happy God — my heavenly Father.

Jesus said that those who saw him saw the Father (Jn. 10:30). And before he was ready to confront the cross he told his disciples "These things I have spoken to you, that my joy may be in you, and that your joy may be full." (Jn. 15:11). Many of us recall that the fruit of the Spirit is love, joy, peace . . . . Think of that! The fruit that our Lord's Spirit nurtures in us is joy. That's because joy is a characteristic of our Father, his beloved Son and the Holy Spirit.

One of the most amazing statements about our beloved Father is recorded in the book of Zephaniah. This Old Testament prophet says of our Lord

The LORD your God is in your midst, a mighty
one who will save; he will rejoice over you with
gladness; he will quiet you by his love; he will
exult over you with loud singing.
(3:17).

Does that thought excite you? Can you perceive your
beloved Father taking great delight in you? Can you envision
him singing a love song to you? Perhaps a lullaby like a parent
lovingly singing his child to sleep at night? That is the picture
Zephaniah is painting for us of our gracious Father's enduring
delight over his darling children.

**Father is absolutely faithful to his promises. His commit-
ment to us will never be broken.**

Probably the first gigantic hurdle a child has to decide is
whether he can trust those who are around him. Through these
relationships he decides whether he can trust the world in which
he lives. And in time he decides whether he can trust the Father
he cannot see. The Psalmist tells us that this Father is absolutely
dependable — utterly faithful.

David lived his life as a warrior. He faced more enemies
than we will ever face. Saul hunted him like a criminal even
though David was a loyal soldier. When he became king he had
to subdue formidable foes. But when he considered these issues
in the Psalns he said that "Some trust in chariots and some in
horses, but we trust in the name of the LORD our God." (20:7).
A few chapters later he affirms that our Lord's faithfulness
reaches to the skies (36:5). And still later we are told that his
faithfulness extends to all generations (119:90). Our Father's
integrity is beyond question.

When my son, Joel, was about four years old I'd stand him

on a four-foot pedestal at the foot of our stairway. Then I'd step back four or five feet and say, "Joel, jump and I'll catch you." Without hesitation my son would leap into open space, confident that my strong arms would catch him before he'd crash to the floor. It is probably no surprise to you to know that I never failed to catch my son. I never thought, "I'll play a trick on him this time and let him fall to the ground." And I never put him in a position in which I couldn't catch him. His trust in me was too precious to violate.

In our humanity we fail each other. Individuals are sometimes hurt when we don't follow through on our promises. But we belong to a Father who will never fail to honor his promises because faithfulness is an essential part of who he is. There is never the question in our Father's mind, "Should I be faithful?" It's always. "I will be faithful." As we entrust ourselves to this unfailing faithfulness the Psalmist assures us that:

- his unfailing love will never end.
- his forgiveness for our sins will continue without end.
- his mercy will be poured out on us without limit.
- his watch care over us will go on night and day, years without end.

Father loves us unconditionally.

What a profound truth! To belong to one who will never withdraw his love from his children.

How comforting to know that we will never be abandoned or forsaken no matter what the circumstances. That's why the Psalmist can boldly proclaim, "Because your steadfast love is better than life, my lips will praise you." (63:3). He is so overwhelmed by this reality that he cannot restrain himself from exalting and praising our beloved Father.

Imagine that!

A love that exceeds life! A love that is worth more than anything or any person on planet Earth could offer us.

It is this enduring love that sold him on his Lord's faithfulness. He knew that he could entrust his life to him because he has come to know the unlimited scope of his love. His way of expressing it is "How precious is your steadfast love, O God! The children of mankind take refuge in the shadow of your wings." (36:7).

At least 29 times in the Psalms we find the word translated unfailing love. In the New American Standard Bible it is translated lovingkindess. It is a word almost exclusive to the Psalms and is used consistently to speak of this unique love that our Lord extends to his people. The Psalms use this word to underscore what the rest of the Bible teaches. Our heavenly Father has an intensely passionate love for his children that defies rational comprehension. I will not be able to grasp how he could love a person like me but the Bible makes it crystal clear that within his heart is an unquenchable love for us that will never diminish.

My own life has been transformed by this incredible profile of a loving Father that radiates everywhere from the writers of the Psalms. Prior to the study of the Psalms I have related earlier in this chapter my view of my heavenly Father was one of discouragement. It seemed as though I never could satisfy him no matter what I tried. I was always seeing failure and it upset him (That's how it appeared in my faulty paradigm). But in my study I came to a verse that struck my mind like a thunderbolt. In the 145th Psalm I read, "The LORD is gracious and merciful, slow to anger and abounding in steadfast love."(v. 8). In my notebook I wrote down each of the four statement as a separate thought.

- my heavenly Father is gracious
- my heavenly Father is compassionate

- my heavenly Father is slow to anger
- my heavenly Father is rich in love

As I meditated on the reality of each statement it became obvious that this snapshot did not square with the one within me. So in the days that followed I'd experience my old paradigm way of thinking I'd prayerfully say, "Father, I realize that right now I'm feeling like you're mad at me and don't want me around. But your word says that you are gracious, compassionate, slow to anger and rich in love and I choose to believe that instead of trusting my feelings."

I followed this process for months. Gradually I found that my inward thoughts and feelings began to align themselves with the truth that the Word of God spoke about. That procedure has been a significant part of the Spirit's transformation process in my life.

OUR FATHER'S HEART EXPOSED

Perhaps you've heard the statement, "The God of the Old Testament is a God of wrath whereas the God of the New Testament is a God of love." My investigation of the Psalms clearly demolished that myth. There is as much expression of our Lord's passionate and compassionate heart in the Old Testament as in the New. His lovingkindness has always been the essence of who he is in every generation.

Just as I've identified an Old Testament source that demonstrates a profile of our beloved Father I'd like to suggest a New Testament parallel. It is a parable that Jesus told which reveals the depth of our Father's love, and gives four expressions of how he relates to us. The parable I'm referring to is found in Luke 15:11-32 and is what is traditionally called the parable of the prodigal son. It is probably more accurate to speak of it as the parable of the father's heart.

One key to understanding this parable is to note the context in which it is given. It is described in verses 1-3. The religious elite were disturbed because unsavory individuals were hanging around Jesus and it didn't seem to disturb him. In fact, he welcomed them. The context suggests that he was at ease in their presence and they enjoyed being with him (Since he is God the Son what does this indicate about how God feels about people?).

As a result of the religious elite's being upset with his association with "losers" Jesus told the three parables in Luke 15. Especially in the third parable we see a more detailed portrait of our Father's heart.

In the account Jesus tells of a son who is discontent with living at home so he appeals to his father to give him what would be due of his inheritance so he can go out and experience life. To our amazement the father complies with his request and off the son hurries to live the life of wine, women and song. But as so often happens the money runs out, the "friends" run out, and the son is left pretty much a beggar. When he hits the bottom he decides to return home and seek employment as a hired hand on the farm. I find in the father's response four characteristics of our heavenly Father.

Father is always seeking us.

As Jesus relates the event he says that the prodigal's father sees him "while he was still a long way off" (v. 20). It doesn't seem logical that the father just happened to see his son coming home. Rather I believe that Jesus is suggesting that our heavenly Father's heart is a seeking heart, always looking out for family members, eager to have them come home to sit at the family table. In my paradigm it seemed as though my Father was fed up with me and would just as soon have me leave. In Jesus' paradigm our Father is never satisfied to have us away from "home" and is constantly reaching out to draw us back to his heart.

Father is unashamed in his tender feeling for us

A second truth that comes through powerfully in this account is the intensity of the father's feelings. Jesus says that the father was filled with compassion toward the son. The word translated compassion is literally a "gut feeling" for his son. This is a very emotional event for the father. Without question Jesus is stressing the father's compassion.

- "he was filled with compassion for him"
- "he ran to his son"
- [he] "threw his arms around him"
- [he] "kissed him"

Notice that each of the four statements is a powerful indication of intense compassion. This picture is consistent with the entire Bible when ever our Father's loving heart is displayed. Even the prophet Hosea revealed the intensely passionate heart of our Father. Speaking through this prophet he said of wayward Israel, "How can I give you up, Ephriam? How can I hand your over, Israel? How can I treat you like Admah? How can I make you like Zeboiim? My heart is changed within me; all my compassion is aroused. I will not carry out my fierce anger, nor will I turn and devastate Ephriam" (Hosea 11:8).

In a way that defies our comprehension our Father consistently demonstrates genuine feelings of compassion for those who are hurting, those filled with shame, those who feel failure, those who are lonely and those who grieve. He is not a detached landlord who is only interested in keeping his property clean and getting his rent paid on time. Rather he is passionate about his children. He loves them, feels their pain and offers intimate compassion.

Father is patient with our failure and sin; he is quick to forgive.

The father's attitude and actions concerning his son's sin is mind boggling. I've often given adults a "prodigal" case study couched in a contemporary situation. Most frequently adults are not willing to welcome a wayward child home without some indication of repentance or remorse, or some guarantees that the parent will not be exploited or humiliated again.

We observe several features of the father's forgiveness. First, he focuses on restoration, not condemnation. All his actions are directed to assure the son that he is being received with joy. Second, he chooses not to give the son what he deserved and gives him what he doesn't deserve. Amazing actions which indicate a grace-filled heart in the father that acts in a way that we'd not expect. Third, his forgiveness frees the son to be honest about his own actions. By extending the spirit of forgiveness in all his actions the son knew that there was no need to defend himself. He could admit his sin and failure because he knew that he would not be condemned.

Father is always relationally generous.

One of the profound acts of the father is to freely give his son those things that would restore him relationally. The robe covered his shame, his ragged clothing. The ring would reaffirm his family identity. The sandals would prove that he would not be treated as a slave, but as a family member. And perhaps the most significant act of generosity was the feast of celebration. It would indicate in a tangible way the father's constant love for his son. He was overjoyed to have his beloved son back home.

I've used the word relationally generous to indicate the difference between those gifts and acts which affirm the pricelessness of our relationship, and those which are merely social courtesies, or obligations for birthdays, anniversaries and holidays. Our Father gives gifts which demonstrate the heartfelt love he has for us, and those things which demonstrate the special place we have in his heart.

DO YOU KNOW HIM?

I once heard a preacher preach a sermon that he entitled, "Your God May Be My Devil." His point was that the perception some people have of our Father better fits the Satan. The evil one is heartless, demanding, dehumanizing, insensitive, unforgiving, etc. Yet some of us have a paradigm that says these are characteristics of our heavenly Father. How crucial to have a proper profile of this profoundly loving, forgiving, encouraging Father. You may find yourself challenged to review what you believe about him and reflect on the perspective the Word of God gives us.

FOR REFLECTION

1. What have your thoughts and feelings been about your heavenly Father? Write them out here.

2. What people or experiences have shaped your view of your heavenly Father? Explain.

3. What ideas in this chapter have challenged your thinking? Why?

11.
CONDEMNED BY
MY CONSCIENCE

*Michael the archangel assigned me to be a guardian angel to this
Caryl. She doesn't realize how much her mind has been filled
with a mixture of truth, half truth, lies, fairy tales, fears, etc.
She is at the mercy of a confused, warped conscience. It's easier
to guard her from an auto accident than to guard her from the
confusion of her thinking. She's vulnerable to all sorts of suggestions and has little peace and tranquility. She reads the Bible, but
then the lies that reside in her conscience create doubt about what
she's read.*

*These followers of Jesus confuse me. Why can't they accept the
clear statements in their Bible about the Sovereign One? Why
can't they rest in him? I'm bewildered.*

— Diary of a Puzzled Angel

THE PROBLEM OF CONSCIENCE

My wife likes to read mystery novels. She especially likes those that keep her in suspense until the very end. She has to guess who the villain is and often finds them in different disguises. One may be charming, another may be openly evil. But since evil people can be dressed in different costumes they are not always easy to spot.

In our study we investigated our formidable foe, Satan. We found him a powerful, clever, persistent, vicious, and well prepared enemy. One of his clever strategies is to create an attractive lie to parallel every truth of our Lord. The uninformed or tempted person is easily attracted to the lie. So often Satan's lies appear to be an easy way to resolve a dilemma, or get out of a scrape. Often they seem logical, sensible and practical. But because they are lies the results are often disastrous and we find ourselves more deeply mired in a situation. It's like the man who believes that he can get what he wants by continuing to use his credit cards without limit. But a time comes when he finds himself hopelessly in debt with no way out.

Underlying this issue is the problem of our conscience.

What comes to your mind when you hear the word "conscience?" We may have a dictionary definition, but it's more important to have a working understanding that helps us in our daily life.

One way I've found helpful to think about our conscience is to recognize that we have two belief systems — an "above ground" belief system and a "below ground" belief system.

The above ground belief system is the thoughts and convictions that I am consciously aware of. It is composed of ideas and concepts that I can rationally discuss and think through with clear logic. But sometimes we fail to realize that parallel to this is another belief system. The "underground" belief system (or conscience) powerfully influences our choices and behaviors and is composed of those thoughts, ideas and emotions that are working in our subconscious mind. This underground belief system motivates my actions for good or for evil. It often consists of ideas, emotions and behaviors that I am not consciously aware of. Perhaps you've heard a person say, "I don't understand why I do that. It seems to come out without even thinking." He is acknowledging an underground influence shaping his emotions and behavior.

The Word of God recognizes our underground belief system—our conscience. When Paul writes to the Corinthian church about Christians eating meat offered to idols he says that the issue involves one's conscience. Listen to his words:

> However, not all possess this knowledge. But some, through former association with idols, eat food as really offered to an idol, and their *conscience*, being weak, is defiled. Food will not commend us to God. We are no worse off if we do not eat, and no better off if we do. But take care that this right of yours does not somehow become a stumbling block to the weak. For if anyone sees you who have knowledge eating in an idol's temple, will he not be encouraged, if his *conscience* is weak, to eat food offered to idols? And so by your knowledge this weak person is destroyed, the brother for whom Christ died. Thus, sinning against your brothers and wounding their *conscience* when it is weak, you sin against Christ. (I Cor 8:7--12 emphasis added)

Paul tells us that some followers of Christ have a weak conscience. That person doesn't know how to discern what is true
from what is untrue and this will lead him to do something that
will bring hurt the his life. Paul also tells us that we can wound
another person's conscience by our actions, and he says that
when I do it, it is a sinful action.

The New Testament defines conscience as the faculty in
us which "distinguishes between what is morally good and
what is morally bad, prompting to do the former and shunning
the latter; commending the one, condemning the other."[1] Our
conscience can include a hodge podge of truth, lies, emotions,
fears, etc. The Bible talks about a weak conscience, a defiled
conscience, a wounded conscience, a seared conscience, a good
conscience and a clear conscience.

GAINING A BIBLICAL PERSPECTIVE

Let's look more closely at our conscience, or, underground
belief system, from a biblical perspective.

First, we learn that it *operates actively* within us doing at least
two things. We are told that it is an active, inner voice that tells
us whether what we or others are doing is good or bad.

Paul, writing to the Romans says of certain people that
"They show that the work of the law is written on their hearts,
while their conscience also bears witness, and their conflicting
thoughts accuse or even excuse them" (Rom. 2:15). Later he describes the active witness of his own conscience when he says, "I
am speaking the truth in Christ—I am not lying; my conscience
bears me witness in the Holy Spirit" (9:1). We are also told our
conscience causes us to judge ourselves and others. "I do not
mean your conscience, but his. For why should my liberty be
determined by someone else's conscience?" (I Cor. 10:29)

I recall having a conversation with a Christian about the forgiveness of sins. The person said, "I've confessed my sins, but I don't feel forgiven. I still feel that God is angry at me." His underground belief system didn't believe the truth of the Word of God so the man continued to judge himself. For all practical purposes his life was driven by an inaccurate but powerful belief system.

The Bible also tells us that our conscience can be *passive*, acted upon by external sources. It can be morally defiled by outside influences. The Bible say that "to the pure, all things are pure, but to the defiled and unbelieving, nothing is pure; but both their minds and their consciences are defiled." (Titus 1:15). When a person associates with emotionally and spiritually unhealthy individuals he begins to pick up thoughts and attitudes that penetrate to the underground belief system and his conscience becomes defiled. Perhaps you can think of someone you know who began to be influenced by unsavory people, and now that individual is enslaved by polluted thoughts.

I recall a conversation with a young Christian who told me that during his teenage years he and his buddies would watch horror movies. "Now I find those images returning at odd hours and it frightens me," he said. Though years had passed he still had internal images and emotions that would arise spontaneously at odd moments. When the conscience is bombarded with lies and deceit it begins to be filled with destructive external influences. Paul was addressing this kind of issue with the Corinthians when he said that a person's weak conscience could be defiled. Many individuals who were originally taught to be sexually pure have allowed their minds and consciences to be defiled and now engage in immoral behavior. They listened to others and their conscience became weakened resulting in carelessness about the choices they make.

The Bible gives us a graphic picture when it tells us that our conscience *can be seared*. The analogy is that of the imprint of a branding iron being burned into the hide of an animal. But Paul applies it to ungodly lies being burned into our minds. We have also noted that a person's conscience can be weakened by the influence of another. One of my daughters took a class at a state university entitled, "The Bible as Literature." The professor's goal focused on creating doubt and suspicion in the minds of his students as to the reliability and trustworthiness of the Bible. Fortunately my daughter responded aggressively, choosing to do research and personal investigation of the facts and her conscience was strengthened, but other students came away with less confidence in the truth of the Scriptures.

The good news is that our conscience can also be influenced for good. It can be cleansed. The writer to the Hebrews says, "how much more will the blood of Christ, who through the eternal Spirit offered himself without blemish to God, purify our conscience from dead works to serve the living God." (Heb 9:14). A bit later he challenges his listeners with the words, "let us draw near with a true heart in full assurance of faith, with our hearts sprinkled clean from an evil conscience and our bodies washed with pure water." (10:22). When Jesus said that "You shall know the truth and the truth shall set you free" (John 8:32), he was laying down a life principle that a person who is committed to discover biblical truth and let it guide his conduct will find a life of freedom and joy.

THE CHALLENGE WE FACE

The challenge before us is to bring our above ground belief system and our below ground belief system into congruence. Many of us know truth intellectually, but it has never filtered down into the underground system in a manner that has "converted" those unhealthy or untruthful beliefs. Consequently we may be able to verbalize the right answers, but subtle whispers of doubt keep arising. So we find ourselves powerless to live them out from a good heart and clear conscience.

What are we to do?

We can begin by being honest with ourselves that we have an unhealthy conscience in certain areas of our life. Until we come to that place we won't challenge those unhealthy, deceitful lies that motivate our behavior and rob us of our Lord's intended joy. One day I realized that I was allowing distorted thoughts to control my life and undermine my joy. I determined that by the strength of the Spirit of God I would not allow this kind of thinking to persist. I began to actively challenge the enslaving lies.

That led me to a second decision.

I realized that the truth that would set me free was the eternal, unchanging truth of what my Lord had said. . .truth found in the Word of God. So I began to think through specific biblical truths that discredit the lies I'd been allowing to control my life. By specific I mean that I went to particular verses and passages and identified them as truths that I would choose to bring against the lie. So whenever the lies arose in my mind or feelings I'd pray something like this: "Lord, right now I'm feeling that you don't like me and are mad at me because I'm not able to be perfect. I recognize that this is not true because your Word says, 'The Lord is gracious and compassionate, slow to anger and abounding in lovingkindness.' (Psa. 145.8). Father, I choose to believe that what you've said is the truth and I now reject the lie that is undermining my peace."

When I began to faithfully apply this process I began to notice that my underground thoughts and feelings slowly began to come into alignment with my above ground thinking—thinking that was based on my Lord's truth. It has motivated me to be sure that I know what my Lord's truth is. So much of what we hear today comes from someone else. Even the preacher's message isn't adequate unless it points me to specific Scripture that I can internalize and use against the lies or deceit to which my conscience has fallen prey. Purposeful, deliberate Bible study should lead me to a cleansed conscience and a harmonious, peaceful disposition that rules my life.

It is also important to evaluate who is influencing my thinking. The Psalmist recognized this when he wrote, "Blessed is the man who walks not in the counsel of the wicked, nor stands in the way of sinners, nor sits in the seat of scoffers" (Psa. 1:1). He understood the destructive impact these kinds of people have on us when we are constantly under their evil influence. But the writer goes beyond this to say, "but his delight is in the law of the LORD, and on his law he meditates day and night."

Do you see the two separate actions the Psalmist is recommending. One, I rid myself of the evil, destructive influences, Two, I replace them with consistent bathing in the Word of God, allowing its truths to penetrate deep within until they shape our thinking and feeling. The Psalmist then describes the kind of person we become—a healthy, fruitful, thriving individual who has great stability in life.

Do you recall what we saw in chapter two about the Evil One's approach to Eve in the Garden of Eden? He polluted her mind with lies about her Lord. Remember, that is his basic strategy to get our relationship off track with our heavenly Father.

I trust that you can see by now that a person with an unhealthy conscience will have difficulty relating to our Lord with freedom and openness. Lies, half-truths, shame, guilt and any other information or emotions that influence our "underground belief system" will push us away from intimacy with our Lord. Just as some in the Corinthian church didn't have freedom in what to eat, so we may have formed attitudes and feelings that are not based on biblical truth. These can twist or distort our underlying beliefs about who our Lord is, what he expects of us, and the freedom he extends to us. He has clearly stated his loving thoughts and feelings toward us, and he has stated his commitment to lead us into holy living. Rooting out the lies, unhealthy emotions and attitudes in our conscience and allowing it to be transformed by truth is an important aspect of our knowing our beloved Father intimately.

FOR REFLECTION

1. What unhealthy thoughts or feelings are controlling important parts of my life?

2. Who has, or is presently, influenced my thinking? What unhealthy concepts or outright lies have I allowed to shape my underground belief system?

3. Do I know clear, specific biblical truth that can counteract these lies? Who could help me find them?

4. What unhealthy influences do I need to cut off from my life?

12.
A FRIEND THAT STICKS CLOSER THAN A BROTHER

I've come to love these children of my Sovereign. The more I get to know them the more I'm puzzled at their understanding of him. Do they not know that the Sovereign One has fully equipped them to face the challenges, attacks and hardships that they will face in their earthly journey? Do they not know that he has sent his Spirit to dwell in them? I am bewildered why Jesus followers vainly do so much in their own energy as though that was what their eternal Father expected. Don't they know that their own strength is totally inadequate for the challenges they will face?

— Diary of a Puzzled Angel

CONFUSED BY MIXED MESSAGES

"But I say, walk by the Spirit, and you will not gratify the desires of the flesh."
Gal. 5:16

In the years that I've known the Lord I've had conversations with many people concerning their walk with our Lord. I've noticed that there are certain issues which troubled them and kept them from developing intimacy with him. Ramona told me of her battle with patterns of sin and how the sense of defeat creates a barrier to intimacy. In a conversation with Ray he said that he grew up in a family that expected perfection in everything and now he has that haunting sense that his heavenly Father expects no less. He gets discouraged when he knows that he can never measure up to this standard. He feels that his Lord is disappointed in him and holds him at arm's length.

Conversations like this have motivated me to understand our Lords ways and be clear in my own mind about what the Word of God teaches on these vital matters. One issue that I had to clarify in my own mind was how the Holy Spirit interacts with my life, what my part is and what his part is. I've also found that I wasn't alone--this is an issue that many Christians are unclear about. Unfortunately one hears a lot of messages that confuse rather than clarify the matter. Many years ago I was a young Christian in the Navy wanting to live closer to our Lord. I was talking with a fellow sailor and he described an experience he had with the Lord that was highly emotional. I came away wishing I could have had the same encounter. But as I've reflected on this over the years and with better perspective I realize that I was looking for an emotional experience to validate my Lord's love for me. If he had given me what I wanted

I would have lived from emotional experience to emotional experience rather than by trusting what he said. Now I'm grateful that I didn't get what I hungered for.

A wise writer some years ago spoke about this matter.

> Right here note that in our search for the conditions of the gift of the Holy Ghost we have confined ourselves too closely to the apostolic experience instead of the apostolic teaching, at Pentecost. Now a man's experience of conversion may be most marvelous and impressive in its accompaniments. But many a man who has had a genuine, glorious experience of conversion utterly fails when he tries to lead others to Christ. Why? Because he imparts into his directions to the anxious seeker conditions from his own experience which are not essential scriptural conditions for others.[1]

The promise of the Holy Spirit's companionship with us in our daily experiences of life is an incredible promise. We need to be clear about the terms and conditions of this relationship. It is crucial that we don't complicate it by adding conditions that our Lord never said were a part of the relationship. In addition, we need to be certain of what he has promised and trust him to be faithful to fulfill his word.

CLARIFYING THE TRINITY

Let's begin with the larger picture of Father, Son and Spirit. It is easy to be vague about each person and not understand the unique place each has in relation to each other, and in relationship to us. Getting the distinctions clear helps us know how to relate to each person of the godhead in a clear and meaningful way. When I'm unclear about the grounds of the relationship I won't be able to enjoy it as much. To gain clarity we will raise some fundamental questions that can guide our thinking.

#1: What do we know about the nature and purpose of the trinity?

First, let's understand that each person of the trinity has a place and purpose for our lives. For example, the Bible tells us that Jesus Christ intercedes for us at the right hand of our Father. So we have one at the very closest position to our heavenly Father who is there representing you and me in our needs and interests. But we are also told that the Spirit of God lives within us and he too intercedes for us, expressing to our Father things that we don't even know how to articulate. So in the wisdom of our Lord we are covered in Father's presence by our Lord Jesus, and we are also covered internally by the Spirit of God who helps us pray when we don't even know how to.

Second, each member of the trinity plays an essential part in the maturing of our lives. Our heavenly Father gives us the place of family identity. He is the head of the family and we have a clear knowledge that we are cherished children (I John 3:1). Our Lord Jesus is the one who settled the issue of our sin so that we can live joyous, freedom-filled lives. He is our glorious King whom we follow. He is the Head of the Church, guiding, coordinating and inspiring us to live in unity. And the Holy Spirit is the empowering presence living within us who fills us with the life and nature of God and equips us to live within the family.

It's important to realize that we need to know how to relate to each member of the trinity to get the full impact of this remarkable relationship. Some people know Jesus as a warm, intimate friend, but have little meaningful sense of a heavenly Father. Others are excited about the Holy Spirit, but don't know an intimacy with the Father and Son. The healthy, balanced child of God will know each member intimately and enjoy the unique place each has in his life.

#2: What do we know about out relationship with our Lord Jesus Christ?

Jesus Christ is the one who made payment for our sins (I Jn 2:1,2). Whenever we think of this issue we think of him. Our heavenly Father is satisfied because Jesus Christ took our place and bore the penalty of our sins. If we wrestle with guilt for our sins we remind ourselves of what he did, turn to him with thankful hearts and give praise for the freedom we have because of him.

The Son of God is also the one who has given us worth (Rom 5:6, 8, 10). Our heavenly Father said that we were worth the life of his beloved Son. Because of his death at Calvary we know that we have high value to our Father.

He is also the one who has given us a remarkable sense of identity. We are a part of the church and he is its Head. He made it possible for us to be drawn into the family and feel loved as a child of the heavenly Father.

#3: What do we know about our relationship with the Spirit of God?

The Bible teaches that the presence of the Holy Spirit living within us brings us supernatural Life. He is the presence of God being lived out through our lives. We express the fruit of the Spirit's presence (Gal. 5, 22, 23), and are invested with supernatural gifts through his residing within our lives (1 Cor 12:4-11).

We also know that the Spirit maintains a low profile (Jn. 16:13, 14). He does not draw attention to himself, but exalts the Father and Son. He works quietly in the background, coming alongside us to strengthen, encourage and equip us, but he does this in a way that honors others rather than himself.

The Spirit is the person who introduces us to the loving heart of our heavenly Father. Paul says that, "Gods love has been poured into our hearts through the Holy Spirit who has been given to us" (Rom. 5:5). One of the great yearning of the Spirit is to flood our hearts with the knowledge of this indescribable love until it becomes a living reality in us.

I've already mentioned that he is the intercessor who lives within us ready to lift every need to the presence of our heavenly Father. He knows us better than we know ourselves. It should encourage us to realize that he can seek our best interests because he knows what our real needs are. Listen to the words of the apostle Paul. "Likewise the Spirit helps us in our weakness. For we do not know what to pray for as we ought, but the Spirit himself intercedes for us with groanings too deep for words. And he who searches hearts knows what is the mind of the Spirit, because the Spirit intercedes for the saints according to the will of God" (Rom. 8:26, 27).

It is one of the Spirit's big purposes to knit each of us together into a spiritual family (I Cor. 12:12, 13). He bears the heart of the Father and Son that there would be incredible unity within the Body of Christ. Christ prayed for this prior to facing the cross. It is his longing that we live in harmony, of one accord. So the Spirit is actively seeking to mold us into one cohesive, interdependent family that is able to accomplish great things that glorify our beloved Father.

Another significant purpose the Spirit of God is accomplishing is to lead us into God's truth (John 14:26, 16:13). He knows that it is truth that sets the child of God free so it is of high priority that we know God's truth and seeing it we see the lies of the evil one that are sown around us. The joyful results of this process are that we experience a renewing of our minds (Rom. 8:5, 6). We see life from a new perspective. Our values and priorities change and we find ourselves living for those things that will outlive our earthly lives.

#4: How do I live in partnership with the Spirit of God?

This is the core issue most of us wrestle with. How do I know him as a Person who lives intimately with me. The preceding verses I cited from Romans 8 makes it clear that he knows me intimately. He knows my longings, my needs, etc. far better than I know them. So he must be intimately connected with me even if I can't see or feel him.

One fact that has helped me know how to relate to the Holy Spirit is to realize that he is a Person. Sometimes when I hear people talk about him it sounds like they are talking about some impersonal force or thing. However, the Bible is clear that the Spirit of God is a person and that tells me something important about relating to him. Because he is a person he can be grieved. Eph. 4:30 says, "Do not grieve the Holy Spirit of God, by whom you were sealed for the day of redemption." Because he is a person he can also be quenched (I Thes. 5:19).

It has helped me to think how I relate to other people. I try to listen to them. I try to treat them with respect. I consider the impact of my attitudes and decisions on them. I try to be considerate of others time. When they seek to help me I express appreciation and allow them to help in a way that they see appropriate.

I have been married for more than fifty years to Winnie. This relationship has thrived for that long because we learned how to interact with each other in loving, gracious, thoughtful ways. It has required me to adjust some of my thinking and change some of my attitudes and behaviors. Because both of us took seriously the commitment we made to each other we learned how to work together, how to enjoy each other's company and how to encourage each other.

Learn to think of your relationship with God's Spirit in the same way. The fact that you can't see him doesn't change the fact of his presence in your life. Treat him as a close intimate friend even though you can't see or feel him. The Bible clearly teaches that he is present, living within you. Learn to act on this truth without depending on some emotional feeling to validate it.

Jesus said, "You will know the truth and the truth will set you free (John 8:32). The truth is that "Now we have received not the spirit of the world, but the Spirit who is from God, that we might understand the things freely given us by God" (I Cor. 2:12). If we have entered into a relationship with Jesus Christ we are promised the Holy Spirit, this intimate companion. Remember he lives with you in a quiet manner, not drawing attention to himself. His interest is for you to know your heavenly Father and the Lord Jesus Christ.

One of the wonderful aspects of this holy relationship is that the Spirit of God wants to empower you to do those things you cannot do yourself. But this requires you and me to stand clear and give him the freedom to act without our stepping in to assert our will, or our demanding that he do things the way we want them. We've been clearly taught that we have a loving Father, that his ways are perfect, that he is a person of ultimate compassions and tenderness, etc. So we need to turn over to his representative, the Spirit, the rights and privileges to lead, teach, empower, and direct our lives as he sees fit. This of course requires that we trust him.

#5: What can I expect to happen in me from this remarkable relationship?

When one entrusts himself to the Spirit of God's loving partnership in my life it is realistic to expect significant changes, though it usually is a growing process over time. Our Lord does things his way and sometimes he makes radical transformations at the time of new birth. For others the new relationship moves more slowly with changes happening gradually, but significant growth occurs according to our Lord's timetable.

All this points up the fact that if godly transformation is to occur we must release control of our lives to him, allowing him to work in the way he knows is best. For most of us this is the crux of the issue. We have learned to operate our lives as seems best to us and it is difficult to relinquish control to another that we cannot see or feel. We have to respond on the basis of truth, not our feelings. But when we genuinely release our lives into his hands positive changes will occur. By positive I mean changes that move us toward godly, fulfilling lives.

Here are some effects we can expect from the Spirit's partnership in our lives. First, we will find ourselves growing in godly wisdom. We will have a clearer perception of ourselves and be wiser about the pressures we feel from those around us. More and more we will discern who our Lord is and his purposes. And we will become wiser in relating to our flesh's demands, the world system in which we live and the evil forces at work in the world.

Second, we can anticipate a growing purity of life. For some this comes through difficulty because our flesh has developed strong addictions to ungodly practices and we find an internal battle between what our flesh wants and what the Spirit of God is working out in us. This is one of the primary places where we must relinquish control of what our flesh wants and allow the Spirit to do what he knows is best.

Third, we can anticipate a deepening love relationship between ourselves and our Lord. The Spirit teaches us about the incredible loving heart the Father and Son have for us. He shows us how to be released from the fears that bind us, and brings us into the loving arms of our Lord. A part of this is learning the truth from the Word of God; a part of it is putting us in touch with the truth about ourselves; a part of it is teaching us how the world, the flesh and the evil one have seduced, robbed and intimidated us. His intention is to set us free from the false loves and the false authorities of our lives.

Fourth, his intention is to lead us into intimate, meaningful communion with our Father. As with other issues this depends on our willingness to have our schedules rearranged, our priorities readjusted and our knowledge of his love for us deepened.

Fifth, we will find his leadership puts us in touch with a new power in our lives. The Spirit bears our Father's authority against sin. The forces of sin must bow to his command. In truth it is his power at work in us, but we have the joyful sense that we are no longer being victimized by illegitimate forces. We find a new power to say "No!" to what is evil, selfish, and corrupt, as well as a new power to say "Yes!" to his love, his resources and his wonderful purposes for our lives.

Sixth, we can expect a growing sense of worship. As we catch a view of his majesty and beauty, as we taste his grace towards us, as we rest in his faithfulness to us, as we come to understand the price he's paid to set us free, as we come to see the indescribable future he has planned for us, we cannot help but lift our hearts to him in heartfelt adoration.

#6: How do I nurture a healthy relationship with this mighty, loving Person?

This loving, kind, faithful Person, the Spirit of God, will be faithful to do all that he has promised. We never have to beg or coerce him to be or do what he has said he will do. Our part is to fulfill the responsibilities that have been given to us. Obviously we need to cultivate a open, teachable heart toward our Lord and his activities within us. Every relationship has two sides. We need to cultivate an honest, intimate relationship. We need to be truthful with our Lord. Sometimes we catch ourselves whining and griping about issues because we want our way, or are unwilling to face difficult challenges

We also need to understand that the beloved Spirit is our greatest ally in the battle against sin. He wants to be the power that delivers us from its evil destruction, but he needs our willing hearts.

We can cultivate a listening heart and a discerning spirit towards this loving Person. He never yells, harasses, or bullies us. He speaks in a quiet, but clear voice if we will listen. We can hear him as we read the Scriptures. We can discern his presence and activities in our life circumstance. At times he will speak through others around us as he works through their lives and their words.

This is a wonderful, warm, intimate relationship that is available to each of us who name the name of Jesus Christ. It is a tragic loss to be invited to know and be led by such an incredible Person and then turn away to lesser concerns. He awaits our friendship; he waits to bless us; he waits to lead us into new, rich experiences. What a partnership!

FOR REFLECTION

1. Do you relate most naturally to God the Father, God the Son, or God the Holy Spirit? Why is this?

2. What do you think you are missing from the other relationships?

3. What in this chapter brought up the most questions in your mind? How will you answer those questions?

4. Read John 13-15. What did Jesus want you to know about his Holy Spirit?

NOTES

Chapter 2: Guilty of Libel

1. Stuart Elliott. "When Doctors, and Even Santa, Endorsed Tobacco." *The New York Times*. October 6, 2008. http://www.nytimes.com/2008/10/07/business/media/07adco.html. Accessed November 19, 2013.

Chapter 3: Filters That Shape Our Perception

1. Edward DeBono. *Serious Creativity*. (New York: HarperBusiness, 1992) 24.
2. Stephen Covey. *Principle-Centered Leadership*. (New York: Simon & Schuster, 1990) 173.
3. Thomas S. Kuhn. *The Structure of Scientific Revolutions*. (Chicago: University of Chicago Press, 1962) 150.
4. Joel Barker. *Discovering the Future*. (St. Paul, MN: ILI Press, 1985) 58.
5. "On This Day: Alexander Graham Bell Granted Patent for Telephone." Findingdulcinea.com. March 7, 2011. http://www.findingdulcinea.com/news/on-this-day/March-April-08/On-this-Day--Alexander-Graham-Bell-Patents-Telephone.html. Accessed December 2, 2013.
6. David Ferguson, Teresa Ferguson, Paul Warren, Vicky Warren. *Parenting With Intimacy*. (Wheaton, IL: Victor Books, 1995) 46.
7. Steve McVey. *Grace Walk* (Eugene, OR: Harvest House, 1995) 16.

Chapter 4: Is Your "Good News" Really Good News?

1. *The American Heritage Desk Dictionary*. (Boston, MA: Houghton Mifflin, 1981) 415.

Chapter 6: How Much is a Penny Worth?

1. "New York Exec Abducted, Rescued." *The Arizona Republic*, August 17, 1993, p. A4.

Chapter 7: Increasing My Capacity to Trust

1. Erik Erikson. *Childhood and Society*. (New York: Norton and Co., 1950).

2. Alan Sieler. "Trust and Relationships." Newfield Institute. http://www.newfieldinstitute.com.au/html/newsarticle011.html. Accessed December 2, 2013.

3. "George Müller My Eye is Not on the Fog." Path2Prayer.com. http://www.path2prayer.com/article/1117/revival-and-holy-spirit/books-sermons/new-resources/famous-christians-books-and-sermons/george-mller-founder-of-bristol-orphanage/george-muller-god-removed-the-fog. Accessed November 19, 2013.

4. Lawrence O. Richards. *Expository Dictionary of Bible Words*. (Grand Rapids, MI: Zondervan, 1985) 113.

Chapter 8: The Real Identity Theft

1. Robert McQuilkin. "Digging Deeper." *Moody Monthly*, March 1993, p. 40.

2. Oswald Chambers. *My Utmost For His Highest*. (Westwood, NJ: Barbour, 1963) 264.

Chapter 9: Love's Many Definitions

1. Chip Ingram, *God: As He Longs for You to See Him*. (Grand Rapids, MI: Baker Books, 2004) 175.

2. Charles Howe, Esq. *Devout Meditations: Or, A Collection of Thoughts Upon Religious and Philosophical Subjects, The Third Edition*. (London: C and J Rivington, 1824). Google eBook edition. http://books.google.com/books?id=OylMAAAAYAAJ&source=gbs_book_other_versions.

Chapter 11: Condemned by My Conscience

1. "Suneidesis." Biblestudytools.com. http://www.biblestudytools.com/lexicons/greek/nas/suneidesis.html. Accessed November 19, 2013.

Chapter 12: A Friend that Sticks Closer Than a Brother

1. James McConkey. *The Three-Fold Secret of the Holy Spirit*. (Pittsburgh, PA: Silver Publishing Society, 1956) 23.

ABOUT THE AUTHOR

Norm Wakefield, Ph.D., is Professor Emeritus at Phoenix Seminary.

He's a former pastor and author of many popular books including, *You Can Have a Happier Family*, *The Dad Difference*, *Solving Problems Before They Become Conflicts*, and *Men are From Israel, Women are From Moab*. Norm is also a father of five adoring children, and much-loved grandfather to eight more kids who think he's really great.

Most of all, Norm Wakefield loves Jesus, and he wants you to share in the joy of Christ's love too.

39486670R00115

Made in the USA
San Bernardino, CA
03 October 2016